Miss Lee Richmond Greenaway
Seaway Farm
Washington, Virginia

Won by Beau Pink
   Junior Horsemanship Class
   Blue Ridge Horse Show
   Millwood, Virginia
  (Miss) Lee R. Greenaway (rider)
   30 Juniors
   Judged throughout whole show
      by secret judges.

Took Family Sure Thing
in Large Pony Division
and got Champion (Reserve)

HORSEMANSHIP

GORDON WRIGHT

and the

UNITED STATES EQUESTRIAN TEAM

Illustrated by Sam Savitt

A primer for the novice: A guidepost for the more advanced

———————A source of review for the expert———————

Copyright, 1958
By Gordon Wright, Tryon, N. C.

All rights reserved, world-wide.

This book, or parts thereof, must not be reproduced in any form without permission.

Printed By The Vermont Printing Company
Brattleboro, Vermont

Binding By Publishers Book Bindery, Inc.
New York, New York

A FOREWORD

By WHITNEY STONE

President, U. S. Equestrian Team, Inc.

AS IN THE CASE of the iceberg, the largest part of competitive international riding lies, unseen, beneath the surface. To the average spectator the performance of a fine team in the Olympic or Pan American Games is a matter of a small handful of outstanding riders mounted on horses that approach or achieve greatness. But, in reality, what he is witnessing is the apex of a great and widespread effort.

As the U. S. Equestrian Team approaches the end of its first decade of existence, this becomes more and more apparent. To produce that necessary handful of top riders and horses so vital to our aspirations in the field of international competition, we must depend upon a broad base of support throughout the entire sport.

Thus, to foster and encourage the development of capable, well-taught riders is more than just a pleasant dream for the U.S.E.T. It is an absolute necessity. If we are to take our proper place among the world's great riding nations, we must be able to look to a vast pool of young riders who enjoy a solid background of well-founded, meticulously-taught horsemanship.

In consequence, the U.S.E.T. must turn hopefully, and even prayerfully, toward those who are engaged in teaching riding.

The implication is clear.

In the long run, the success of the U.S.E.T. will be in direct ratio to the quality of instruction available to that tremendous number of young riders from which our future Olympic and International teams will be chosen.

Not the least of this country's natural resources is the presence of teachers of the caliber of Gordon Wright. His personal qualifications are so well known that they need no review here.

Through his personal efforts as a teacher and through the medium of his written works, he has contributed widely to the progress of equestrian sport in this country.

Now he has, in this book, made another extremely valuable contribution to the riding game. Here is a work that pursues the continuity of his efforts through the years—a book that can only enhance the efforts of the thoughtful student of the art of riding.

For the comparative novice, Gordon Wright has written a book which can set his feet correctly upon the path to riding proficiency. For the more advanced, it can serve as a check and a solid guidepost. And for the expert, it enjoys the virtue of being a worthwhile source of review and reference.

It is my conviction that this is a book which will not only be of extreme value to all students of riding but one which will, in the final analysis, materially aid the cause of the U.S.E.T.

Whitney Stone

New York, New York
1958

PREFACE

WHEN THE UNITED STATES Equestrian Team agreed to join with me in this new book, I experienced one of the truly proud moments of my career. Based on the outcome of show after show, it is written in the record that these young men have done much to increase the quality of horsemanship. Obviously they have much to contribute in the pages that follow.

And yet, I am proud to be associated with them and my other co-authors in this volume for an equally important, if less tangible reason. Together, they have demonstrated the high caliber of their sportsmanship to millions of people here and abroad. It is the belief of the author that this book which combines our respective experiences—theirs in present day international competition and mine in many years of productive teaching and showing—will be a worthwhile addition to progressive horsemanship in our country.

Gordon Wright

THE ROYAL INTERNATIONAL HORSE SHOW

White City Stadium, London

JULY 24, 1958

THE EDWARD, PRINCE OF WALES CUP

International Team Jumping Competition

(Prix de Nations)

The most coveted team trophy in the world is shown on the slip-case of this book. Each nation enters 4 horses. Each horse must jump the exacting course of some 15 obstacles, ranging from 4 ft., 6 in. to 5 ft., 3 in. twice. Length of course about 900 yards (approximately ½ mile).

The cup was first competed for in 1920 and up to the 1958 show, Great Britain won it on 16 occasions — France 5 — Italy 3 — Ireland 1 — and U.S.A. 1.

Won by U.S.A. in 1958 —— Great Britain reserve.

THIS BOOK IS RESPECTFULLY DEDICATED
TO THE MEMORY OF A GREAT MAN AND GOOD FRIEND
WHO WAS EQUALLY DEDICATED
TO THE CAUSE OF HORSEMANSHIP
GEORGE S. PATTON, JR.
GENERAL, UNITED STATES ARMY

TABLE OF CONTENTS

SECTION ONE—Training the Rider—First Grade

Horse Sense	3
Learning To Learn	4
Mounting	6
Dismounting	7
Position	8
Reins	13
Aids	15
Jumping	20

SECTION TWO—Stable Management

Part I	Grooming	29
	Equipment	33
Part II	Cleaning Track by Robert Freels, Stable Manager, U.S.E.T.	41
	Bandaging by Robert Freels	42
	Braiding by Robert Freels	44

SECTION THREE—The Rider—Second Grade

Part I	Reins	49
	Aids	51
	The Posting Trot	53
	Turns	59
	Schooling	62
	Jumping	70
	Showing the Hunter	72
Part II	Longeing by Bertalan de Nemethy, Coach, U.S.E.T.	73
Part III	Fox Hunting by Mrs. John J. McDonald, Ex-MFH, Meadowbrook Hunt	80

SECTION FOUR—The Horse

Part I	Head	89
	Leg	90
	Color Guide	90
Part II	Selecting A Horse	91
	Conformation	94
Part III	Unsoundness	95
Part IV	Veterinary Preparation of the Horse and Maintenance of Condition During Competition by Dr. Joseph C. O'Dea	102
	Pain Killers and Tranquilizers by Dr. Joseph C. O'Dea	105

SECTION FIVE—The Rider-Expert

Part I	The Employment of Cavalettis by Bertalan de Nemethy, Coach, U.S.E.T.	111
Part II	Flexions and Collections	114
	Jumping	120
	F.E.I.	123
Part III	The Three Day Event by Brig. Gen. John T. Cole, U.S.E.T.	125
Part IV	Analyzing Jumping Courses by William Steinkraus, Captain, U.S.E.T.	129
	Time Classes by Frank Chapot, U.S.E.T.	143
Part V	The Olympic Games by Maj. Gen. Guy V. Henry, U.S. Olympic Equestrian Committee	145

LIST OF ILLUSTRATIONS

SECTION ONE

Horse Sense	3
Mounting	6
Dismounting	7
Position	8
Correct Position of the Leg	12
Holding the Single Rein	13
Holding the Double Rein	14
Leading Rein	14
Direct Rein	15
The Canter	19
Jumping, First Stage	20
Jumping, First Grade	22, 23

SECTION TWO

Grooming	29
To Pick up a Hind Foot	30
To Pick up a Front Foot	31
To Clean out the Feet	32
Plain Snaffle	36
Halter	36
Pelham	36
Breastplate	36
Wire Snaffle	37
Double Bridle	37
Bridling the Horse	38
Standing Martingale	38
Running Martingale	39
The Saddle	40
Braiding	44

SECTION THREE

Indirect Rein	49
Pulley Rein	50
Draw Rein, Drop Nose Band	50
Posting Diagonals	55
The Canter	56
The Gallop	57
The Shoulder-In	58
Turn or "Bend"	59
Turn on the Forehand	60
Turn on the Haunches, A	61
Turn on the Haunches, B	62

The Circle	64
The Figure Eight	65
Serpentine	66
The Half Turn	67
The Half Turn in Reverse	68
Broken Line	69
Riding a Course of Jumps	71
Longeing	74
Long Line to Bridle	74
Side Lines or Draw Reins	75
Longeing the Rider	77
Correctly Constructed Saddle	78
Hunting Manners	85

SECTION FOUR

Head Markings	89
Leg Markings	90
Selecting a Horse	91
Regions	93
Unsoundness	95
Pain Killers	105
Tranquilizers	106

SECTION FIVE

Cavalettis	112
Cavalettis and Fence	112
Direct Flexion	114
Lateral Flexion	114
Extended Trot	118
Two Track	119
Jumping	120, 121
Broken Line	122
Someone's Mistake	127
Course for the Olympic Games at Stockholm, 1956	130
Individual Jumps at 1956 Olympic Equestrian Games Used for the Prix des Nations	
1 and 2	132
3	133
4 and 5A	134
5B and 6	135
7, 8 and 9	137
10 and 11	138
12A, 12B and 12C	139
13 and 14	140
Out for Time	144
Olympic Torch	148

SECTION ONE

Training the Rider—First Grade

Horse Sense	3
Learning To Learn	4
Mounting	6
Dismounting	7
Position	8
Reins	13
Aids	15
Jumping	20

ABOUT THE ILLUSTRATOR. A proficient horseman himself, Pennsylvania-born Sam Savitt is one of the nation's leading horse artists, specializing in both portraiture and illustration. Because of his unique abilities as horseman and painter, he was the most logical selection as the official artist for the United States Equestrian Team. It is most interesting to note that horseman Savitt, only a few years ago, trained and schooled a three year old filly named War Bride—who now has the double distinction of being on the U. S. team and becoming a subject for artist Savitt.

TRAINING THE RIDER—FIRST GRADE

Horse Sense

HORSE SENSE is actually the animal's instinct for self preservation. It does not mean intelligence. The average horse's mentality can be compared, not too favorably, with that of a two-year-old child. To the horse, reward is the lack of punishment, in other words—*self preservation*. The horse is one of the most timid of animals physically and is easily frightened by rough handling or an unfortunate experience. There is no such thing as a horse who is not afraid.

The horse has a marvelous memory; it is his greatest mental aptitude. He acquires habits quickly, good or bad, and sticks to them. Consequently the only successful method of horse training is to have the animal obey through the memory of reward.

The horse's individual temperament has a great deal to do with one's method of training and the rider must learn to differentiate between fear and resistance in his horse.

If the horse refuses to obey his rider from fear, the rider must instill confidence. If the horse resists from stubbornness, the rider must quickly show who is master. However, no attempt should be made to punish the horse when the rider has lost his temper because the punishment is bound to be too severe and unconstructive. Such punishment is unnecessary and often cruelly destructive. Always remember, it takes little time to unschool a schooled horse, but it takes endless time and patience to reschool a spoiled horse.

A young horse is often shy about coming to a human and may be difficult to catch when turned out to pasture. This shyness can be overcome by the reward of carrots or a piece of sugar each time he is caught. Eventually, he will come when called of his own accord. Again, many horses, as the result of some unfortunate occurrence are head shy and practically impossible to bridle. Instead of force, fasten a carrot to the bit so that he wants to take it. By doing this fifteen or sixteen times in one day, I have cured the worst case of head shyness in my experience. However, never feed tidbits to your horse promiscuously. He will learn to expect a handout from any passer-by and become a "nipper", an unpopular and dangerous sort of horse to have around a stable.

As I mentioned earlier, horses have great physical fear. Unfortunately, human beings have to cope with *two* fears, physical and mental. Human physical fear is very difficult to overcome and is easily transferred to the horse who in turn loses his courage. Human mental fear, the fear of not doing well (in other words "pride") very seldom interferes with a horse unless the rider has an extreme case, then he freezes and his controls don't function.

If you have physical fear, remember the horse is more frightened than you. If you have mental fear, remember most of the people in the gallery couldn't do as well as you and wouldn't change places for the world. Be a ham.

Learning To Learn

We are told by educators and psychologists that the process of learning becomes greatly slowed down after the age of twenty five. The validity of this is demonstrated in the fact that children and very young people learn to ride more quickly and easily than do older people. Chief among the reasons for this is the ability of the former to concentrate upon what they are doing. One of the most difficult tasks facing the riding instructor is to get the pupil to fasten his mind upon one thing at a time. The novice, learning to keep his heels down, must forget, for the moment, about his hands.

Until your reactions on a horse have become instinctive and automatic, don't clutter your mind with half a dozen different things to do. By concentrating on one thing at a time until it is automatic, and then going on to master something else, the rider will learn more quickly and be less apprehensive, especially during the early lessons. First, he must have enough confidence in his instructor to do what he is told without question. If the pupil cannot have complete confidence in his instructor, then he is wasting the money he is spending on riding lessons.

When people are learning to ride they often are over-mounted, which may shake their confidence. But, a great deal of the time, they find themselves over-mounted because of false pride which keeps them from admitting to the riding instructor or others how little they ride, or, more important, how hesitant or timid they really feel.

Everyone is hesitant and timid about some horse and some kinds of riding or jumping, no matter how courageous a rider he may be. Because courage can only come from confidence, anyone who has had a bad experience on a horse will lose his confidence, and, therefore, his nerve, temporarily. But, if he has been taught what to do, and if he knows why the accident happened, his confidence can always be restored.

Therefore, don't hurry this early work. Setbacks in the early stages of learning to ride are much worse than setbacks that may come later, when the rider knows the particular risk he has taken, or the more dangerous horse he has ridden because he wanted to ride him. In these early stages, the rider must have only good experiences. He should not fall off; he should never have the experience or the feeling, of a horse out of control; he should finish each lesson or each day's work, with a good feeling, looking forward with real enjoyment, and not in an agony of apprehension, to the lesson to follow.

Confidence

Apprehension is based on fear and fear is based on ignorance. The rider who doesn't know how to stop a horse cannot be expected to show a great deal of courage about getting him started. The rider who is unaware of the reason his horse refused a jump is naturally apprehensive about riding down to that jump again. As his reluctance is quickly transmitted to the horse, another refusal may be expected, and with it will come an even more apprehensive rider.

That is why the early work must not be hurried, either by the over-anxious pupil, the zealous parent, or the ambitious teacher. It is easier to prevent the formation of bad habits, both in horse and rider, than to correct them. The young child mounting a horse or pony for the first time shows no fear. Only bad experiences produce fear and timidity, and most of these can be avoided.

The Pupil Should: Never be apologetic about low jumps or quiet horses. Have confidence in his instructor, or get another in whom he will have confidence.

Allow himself to be told what to do, *not* tell the instructor what he wants to do, or how high he believes he can jump.

Follow a definite sequence of instruction, lesson by lesson and grade by grade. Don't attempt second grade and advance courses before you have completed first grade. Be sure one lesson has been absorbed thoroughly before moving on to the next, and be sure that quiet horses have been mastered before risking confidence and security—to say nothing of riding pleasure and relaxation—by asking for more difficult horses.

The Instructor Should: Never ridicule a pupil's horse, riding ability, or past experience.

Consider a rider's good and bad points in much the same way he would

1. The rider stands half facing the rear, opposite the horse's left shoulder. He takes the reins in his left hand, with the little finger between them and the bight falling to the off side. Adjust the reins so they give a gentle, even bearing on the horse's mouth. Now, place the left hand, with the reins, on the horse's crest. The rider then places his left foot in the stirrup assisted by his right hand, if necessary, and brings his left knee against the saddle. Without pause, he places the right hand upon the cantle.

MOUNTING AN

2. He springs off his right foot, with the aid of his right hand on the cantle of the saddle. He brings the right foot alongside the left and changes the right hand to the pommel.

3. He now passes the right leg, knee bent, over the horse's croup without touching it and sinks down lightly in the saddle. He then places the right foot in the stirrup and takes the reins in both hands.

DISMOUNTING

1. The rider passes the reins into his left hand and places that hand on the horse's crest. He then places the right hand on the pommel of the saddle, removes the right foot from the stirrup, and passes the right leg, knee bent, over the croup without touching it.

2. He now places the right foot alongside the left foot, the left knee being against the saddle and the upper body inclined slightly forward.

3. He puts the weight of his body on his hands, removes the left foot from the stirrup, then descends lightly to the ground.

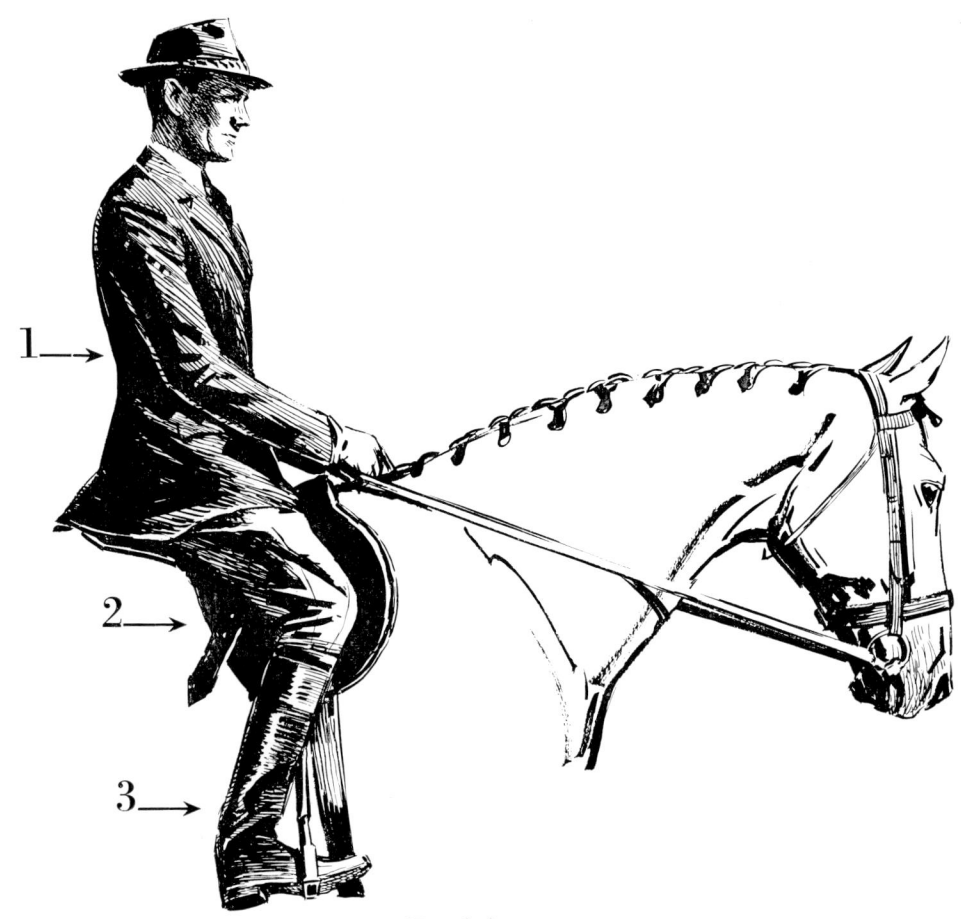

Position

The rider's body is distributed as follows:

Part of the Body	Definition	Position
1. Upper Body	All parts of the body from the hips up.	Eyes forward, back straight; hands over and in front of horse's withers; knuckles thirty degrees inside the vertical; hands two inches apart and making a straight line from horse's mouth to rider's elbow.
2. Base of Support	All parts of the body in contact with horse or saddle.	Crotch deep in the saddle; inner bones of the knees and calves against the horse's sides.
3. Leg	All parts of the leg from the knee down.	Toes out about fifteen degrees, according to rider's conformation; ankles flexed in, heels down, calf of leg in contact with horse and slightly behind girth.
4. Equilibrium	Balance of upper body over the base of support at the different gaits.	At the walk, vertical; slow trot, vertical; posting trot, inclined forward; canter, half way between the posting trot and the walk; galloping and jumping, same as the posting trot.

consider a horse's. There are some conformation faults that limit a rider's ability, just as there are conformation faults that limit a horse's ability. Realize the importance of temperament. There are temperamental differences in people as well as horses. Even if the pupil has proved to be physically capable of doing difficult things, he should not be urged to do so if his temperament is unsuited to the increased nervous tension which naturally accompanies the higher jumps. To ridicule such a pupil, with the mistaken notion that you are appealing to his pride to do what his heart won't do, is as unkind as it is unwise.

Try to avoid having a negative attitude. By this I mean, add to what the pupil already has, instead of trying to start all over again. He *has* a certain horse, he *has* a certain seat, both acquired, in many instances, at considerable expense. It is extremely discouraging to be told he has to get rid of his horse and "forget" everything he has learned. The best and most that the pupil can do is improve on everything he has learned, and in this the conscientious instructor can and should assist him.

Use a regular sequence of instruction, beginning with the correct use of the aids in stopping, then moving on to the correct use of the aids in moving forward and in turning. There can be no seat on a horse until there is control, and no hands until there is a secure seat.

Insist that the work go slowly. There is absolutely nothing to be gained and everything to be lost by hurrying the early work, for no real progress can be made with even the most talented pupil until security has been achieved. Now is the time to give the most important thing to a rider who wants to go on and really do things . . . and that is *Confidence*. Don't risk it until he has it. If he does not, try to build it constructively by seeing that he is not overmounted, or by not asking more than he is capable of doing.

A good position on a horse is one that can be adjusted to the needs of the rider. It should fulfill the two primary requisites of a good seat—a maximum of security for the rider and a minimum of interference for the horse.

The position illustrated here provides these two basic requirements.

If our sole aim were to provide maximum security for the rider, the stirrups would be lengthened drastically, giving the rider more leg. If our sole aim were to provide maximum freedom for the horse, the stirrups would be shortened drastically, taking even more weight off the horse's back and putting the rider more or less in the position of a jockey.

Obviously, both of these exaggerations have severe drawbacks. In the first, the horse's movements are so severely interfered with by the pounding of the rider's weight on his back that his work is made doubly hard, with resultant loss of efficiency and good performance. In the second, the rider has no security and rides, like a jockey, entirely on balance. Therefore, the ideal position on a horse is one that allows the rider full use of all his natural aids—such as the calves of the legs, and the hands,—by placing them in positions where they serve to increase the rider's security in the saddle, while at the same time acting as a means of communication between the horse and the rider.

Anyone who has ever been privileged to observe a horse turned loose in pasture, galloping down to a jump, knows that the free horse does not fall over his fences, "get in wrong," or commit any of the blunders which occasionally make jumping a hazard. All such faults and disasters are generally the result of interference on the part of the rider with the horse's movements. There is some interference which cannot be helped, regardless of the rider's skill or his position in the saddle. A horse stumbles or shies suddenly just before a jump, and the rider is temporarily thrown out of position. It is safe to say that a majority of falls and refusals result from severe—and sometimes constant—interference with the horse due to the rider's faulty or unbalanced position in the saddle.

The position which you see illustrated here is the position which I teach and advocate because it avoids extremes, and has the added advantage of putting the rider into correct jumping position long before he has even begun to walk over a rail on the ground.

I don't believe the average rider has a lifetime to spend learning the fine technicalities of horsemanship. Therefore, insofar as it is commensurate with a rider's safety and a horse's well being, I plan the lessons so that the rider is enjoying the thrills and pleasure of jumping the low jumps within a *very* short time. For the higher jumps, the *rider* does exactly the same things which he does on the lower ones. The difference is that he must have a somewhat better horse, and he must have spent enough hours in the saddle to have built up the necessary security and confidence in himself, and his horse, to be ready to tackle the higher jumps.

Throughout this book, you will observe that I carefully avoid using the word *"nerve"* in its accepted sense, because, as far as riding is concerned, nerve comes from confidence. When a rider has had enough good experiences on a horse, when he has developed confidence in his instructor, which later can and should be transferred first to the horse and then to the rider himself, *every* rider has nerve. The riders who take chances without understanding the risks involved are more foolhardy than courageous.

For this reason, the pupil who is made to control his natural impatience in the early stages of developing a secure seat on a horse will find himself making rapid progress later on when this position has become automatic. You will see, and have seen, a great many fine and successful riders whose position in the saddle defies everything I have said, or will say to you, regarding position. Some people who have exceptionally well co-ordinated and athletic bodies can be any place on a horse, and still manage to be "with" the horse when he takes a jump, by performing truly incredible gymnastics in the saddle at the last minute. They do well, and they succeed. Bear in mind, however, that there are geniuses in every field, and riding is no exception.

To take his position in the saddle: The rider should spend the first five minutes of each of the first fifteen hours of riding adjusting his position in the saddle.

When the different parts of the body have been arranged and distributed as shown and explained in the accompanying illustration and text, the rider stands up in his stirrups, placing one hand in the mane to steady himself. Then he relaxes the ankle joints so the heels, driven by the body's weight, are forced far down, keeping the stirrup straps vertical and the legs in place against the horse's sides. The toes turn out just enough so that the ankles are flexed. Then, holding the lower legs in place, he sinks down slowly into the saddle, with the crotch in the middle of the saddle. This is called the three-point contact. He establishes the two-point contact by standing up in his stirrups, weight in heels, seat out of saddle.

You will find that all horses have some degree of difference in conformation when you are standing up in your stirrups with the correct contact. You feel a large, well-ribbed horse lower down in your calf, whereas the narrow type close to your knee, but never in your knee.

Try to hold this two-point position at the walk, then the slow trot, and finally the fast trot. Just five minutes a day taking and holding this position at these gaits will produce excellent results. Upon completion of the first fifteen hours of riding which have included this simple exercise, the rider will find himself assuming this position in the saddle automatically.

The Difference Between Looking and Seeing

First of all, make sure you know the difference between looking and seeing. Always *look* where you are going, while still *seeing* your horse, the jump, or holes in the ground. It is important to master this exercise. It is the exercise to work at, in conjunction with your controls, to give you automatic reaction. Therefore, when you are learning, resist all temptation to look down. Don't look at the jump and don't peer underneath your horse's belly to see which lead he is on.

Adjust your position a step at a time and don't expect to be able to hold it right away. It takes time, but the period is shortened by not trying to hurry these early stages, thus avoiding pressure, strain, and fatigue.

In learning the correct position of the leg, first study the illustration on the following page; then at a standstill and with your eyes straight ahead, say to yourself, "Toes out at an angle of about fifteen degrees". Your own leg conformation will pretty well tell you what is the comfortable and therefore correct, degree for you. Then, when you think you have it, ask your instructor, or someone who is willing to work with you, to check your position. If you're working alone, a riding hall mirror is almost invaluable, but, if no

CORRECT POSITION OF THE LEG

mirror is available, adjust your position in accordance with your mental picture of what is correct, and *then* look to compare. Your toes control the position of your knees. If toes are out too far, knees will be too far from the saddle.

Next, try "ankles flexed". Again, check on your mental picture of the ideal ankle flexion as shown here, which calls for the ball of the foot to be in the stirrup—but *resting* there, not pressing. Heels should be down, the calf of your leg slightly behind the girth and in contact with your horse. I have no feeling whatsoever about riding "home" or riding on the ball of the foot; but *when the pupil is learning to keep his heels down, it's easier for him to put weight in the heels if he rides on the ball of the foot.* And *do* remember that pressure and weight are carried in the heel, *not on the stirrup.* Pressing on the stirrup has the effect of drawing the rider's calf away from his horse—or his legs too far forward—thereby depriving him of an important means of communicating with, and controlling, his horse, plus lessening the rider's security in the saddle. The same procedure, as outlined above, should be followed for each of the four parts of the body which form your position on the horse.

The importance of not looking down as you adjust the different parts of the body cannot be overstated. Learn from the very beginning to keep your eyes forward, to form a mental picture in your mind. To learn this all-important habit of *looking* and feeling, I recommend that the rider focus his eyes on some point directly ahead of him and on a level with his eyes, so that he can catch himself if he glances down. It is physically impossible to maintain proper balance in the saddle when the eyes are down.

The next time you take a very low jump, try it. First, look down at the jump you are taking, and the next time, determine to keep your eyes forward and still see the jump. You will be astonished at the difference this makes, both in your own position on the horse, *and* the horse's performance over a jump. When the eyes are down, nothing is functioning. The driver who kept his eyes on the steering wheel would soon find himself, and his car, in a ditch. The rider who looks down at his horse will soon find his horse refusing and running out, because when the rider's eyes are down he is *looking* instead of thinking or feeling. Watching a horse take a jump is a good way *not* to have him take the jump.

To Summarize Position: A good position in the saddle is one which provides security for the rider and freedom of movement for the horse. The position illustrated is readily and easily adapted to the requirements of both the hunt field and the show ring.

In adjusting the forward inclination of the body for the different gaits and the higher jumps, remember that forward inclination is controlled by the opening and closing of the hip angles, *not* by collapsing on the horse's neck or rounding the back.

It is the horse's back, loin and hindquarters which furnish the driving power—another good reason why they should be reasonably unhindered. Don't try to learn this position all at once. The temporary loss of security which always accompanies changing old riding habits for new ones, and the slight strain on new muscles being used for the first time, plus the slightest uncertainty on the part of the rider, can all be avoided if the rider will learn this position by practicing only five minutes a day at a walk, a slow trot, and a posting trot.

Repetition is what actually teaches you—doing the same thing again, and again, and again. And repetition, plus making haste slowly, is what you will find most useful for everything—from acquiring a good position on a horse to learning how to jump.

Reins

HOLDING SINGLE REIN: The rein is held in two hands *around* the little finger, passing up through the palms and over the index fingers. The thumbs are placed on top of the reins, placing them against the middle joint of the index finger, which prevents the reins from slipping.

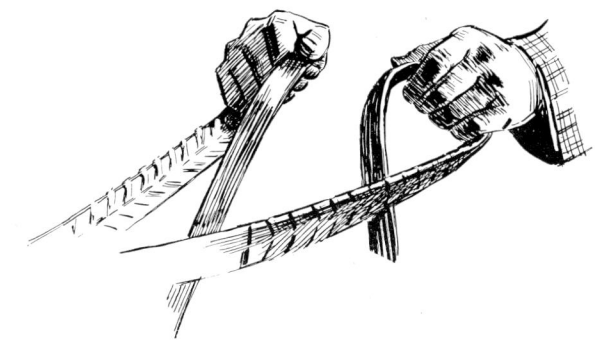

HOLDING DOUBLE REINS: When the reins are held in both hands, the snaffle rein enters each hand *underneath* the little fingers. The curb enters between the little and ring fingers, both reins run up together, passing through the palms, over the index fingers with the thumbs on the reins.

THIS IS A LEADING REIN: It displaces weight on the forehand in the direction of movement. The effect and use is to turn the horse in any direction by leading it. This is particularly useful when working with very young or green horses as the action is a simple one.

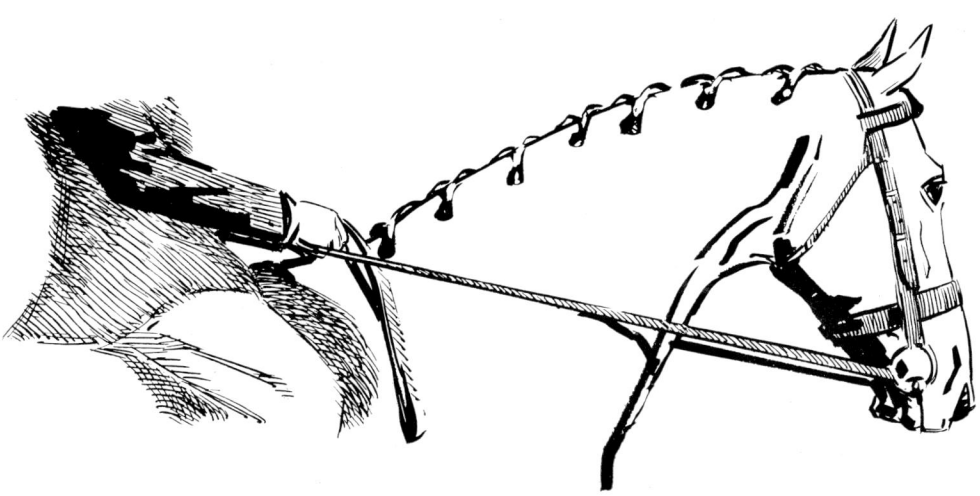

THIS IS A DIRECT REIN: It makes a direct line from horse's mouth to rider's elbow. It is used to control forward motion and to displace the horse's weight from forehand to haunches. It is the rein which is used most often in all riding.

Aids

At this stage the rider should be acquainted with the correct regions on his horse—*near side* is left side; *offside* is the right side; *Forehand*—all parts before and including the withers; *Hindquarters* all parts in rear of loin; *Middle piece* includes back loin, ribs, girth and flank.

Before moving on to the posting trot the rider, to be safe and at ease in the saddle, must have at least an elementary knowledge of the aids used to increase or decrease a horse's forward motion.

The first aids which the rider is called upon to use are the rein aids.

To Decrease Speed: At the walk, the rider, having established light contact with his horse's mouth, closes his hands on the reins. The little fingers of the rider's hands act in a squeezing motion, increasing pressure on the reins and therefore, on the horse's mouth. The horse comes back from the walk to the halt. Do not add any more pressure on the reins than is necessary.

To Move the Horse Forward Again, or Increase Speed: Relax hands, or feel of horse's mouth, then close legs against his sides. The inexperienced rider should *never* be mounted on a horse so sour to the leg that he requires the use of the stronger aids, which if not used judiciously, can cause trouble. In learning the use of the elementary controls, it is important that they be learned at the very slow gaits, while the rider learns to feel the various effects which the different aids produce. He should first move only from the halt to the walk and back to the halt again, until the aids needed for this exercise are functioning smoothly. The rider will relax as he learns he can control speed with little effort.

The rider should never kick his horse. It is not only a most unhorsemanlike sight, but has the effect of popping the rider out of the saddle, precisely as a lemon seed might be popped out by holding the lemon seed tightly between two fingers and squeezing. Kicking the horse disturbs the rider's balance and equilibrium in the saddle. Never ask a horse to do more than you are capable of having him do; and the rider who is just learning the correct use and co-ordination of the aids is certainly not able to insist on obedience from a horse who does not respond to light pressure on the reins or a fairly mild action of the legs. It does not require a good horse to do these things but it does require a good-dispositioned horse. That is the kind of horse you should be on at this stage of your riding education.

Hands

Hands, like reins, are one of the rider's natural aids, and one of the aids he always uses when mounted, whether he is using them voluntarily or involuntarily, skilfully or awkwardly. Good hands do not always follow a good seat but good hands are impossible without a good seat. And by a good seat, I mean a seat that is safe enough and secure enough so the rider never has to go to his reins for support. No horse can be expected to associate the ideas of halting, turning, or decreasing the gait with varying tensions on the reins applied incorrectly.

Horses are born with dispositions that make them either less or more adaptable to training and schooling, but horses are not born with bad mouths. Bad hands make bad mouths, and bad mouths can, in turn, make heavy, if not bad hands in the inexpert rider. For this reason, until the rider has achieved a fair degree of security in the saddle, he should strive only to have steady hands. These are hands that even the rankest amateur can acquire, and reasonably soon, if he will concentrate not on the far-off goal of educated hands, but on the immediate goal of steady hands.

When the legs have asked for an increase in the gait, the rider should be sure that his hands relax sufficiently to allow the horse's head and neck to move freely to accommodate the increased impulsion. After the hands have closed on the reins, asking for a decrease in speed and the horse has obeyed the command, the hands should relax instantly, rewarding the horse for his obedience and making him quicker to respond the next time the signal is given.

A rider may have any one of four kinds of hands on a horse: good hands, by which I mean steady, considerate hands; bad hands, the hands that constantly abuse a horse's mouth by the rider intentionally or unintentionally, urging forward and reining back at the same time; no hands, referring to those riders who habitually ride with excessively long reins, maintaining no contact with the horse's mouth at all; and, finally, the goal of every ambitious rider: educated hands.

It requires a lifetime of riding to acquire really educated hands, because by "educated hands" I mean hands which are fixed on the reins with a resistance *exactly* equal to the resistance of the horse's mouth against them, hands so sensitive they can yield at the very instant the horse yields to their pressure. To continue that severe a pressure in the horse's mouth even an instant longer than is necessary is to continue a punishment *after* the horse has yielded.

Many riders get into the habit of riding with "no hands" through having been cautioned against using too much pressure on a horse's mouth. Too much pressure, produced by the set or heavy hand, is certainly to be avoided, but on the other hand so is the horse whose mouth "can't be touched". All cars come equipped with brakes and all horses should, too. There is something wrong with the horse who cannot or will not respond to the proper application of the rein aid. He is a horse which the inexperienced rider should not be riding.

After security in the saddle has helped the rider to have steady hands, the next step toward the development of good hands is passive hands. These are hands that are able to function independently of the body, that can work separately, in sequence, or simultaneously.

Passive and active hands are used simultaneously, for instance, in turning a horse. Turning to the right, the right hand becomes active, the left hand is passive. Many riders *think* their hands are passive when, actually, they are active. It is important to be sure that the passive hand is really passive when the active hand is active. Human beings have nervous breakdowns when they try to go in two directions at once, yet this physical and mental impossibility is something which the unskilled or thoughtless rider is constantly demanding of his horse whenever he clashes his aids or controls. The rider is said to be clashing his controls when his hands refuse to yield after the legs have asked for forward motion or when a passive hand continues to be active, conflicting with the signal of the active hand; or when an unsteady leg against a horse's side continues to ask for forward motion while the hands continue to increase their feel against his mouth, countermanding the unintentional signal of the legs.

The thing to bear in mind in the development of good hands is that they only follow a secure seat. When learning to ride, forget hands altogether except to take care that the hands are steady enough not to interfere with the horse's mouth and inflict needless pain and punishment. Ride only quiet horses which will respond, either through the medium of good mouth or good disposition, to light and proper pressure on the reins applied by *closing* the hands and *not* by *pulling* on the reins. As the rider's security in the saddle is increased, he should gradually begin to acquire steady hands.

Legs

Just as there are active and passive hands, so too, are the legs either active or passive. Again, care must be exercised to see to it that the passive leg is *really* passive, assisting the action of the active leg and becoming active, only when the horse decreases the speed at which he is moving. Some riders have "no legs" on a horse, because their grip is entirely through the knees and the upper thighs. Such a position may be made to be secure through the medium of strength, balance, and general athletic ability but it is obvious, even to the beginner that when the rider does not bring the calves of his legs in against the sides of his horse, he is sacrificing an important means of control and part of his security.

Every rider needs all the security and control he can get, so that it seems foolish, deliberately and needlessly, to sacrifice this vital part of the seat.

First Grade Backing

The proper way to back your horse with the use of the direct rein: The rider establishes contact with his horse by taking a feel of his mouth, next applies pressure by closing hands, feels the weight from the forehand move to the quarters, and then *waits* for his horse to back.

Speeds at the Different Gaits

You should know the proper speeds for the walk, the slow or sitting trot, and the posting trot.

At the walk, the horse should move approximately four miles an hour; slow trot, six miles an hour; posting trot, eight miles an hour. Horses will trot as fast as thirty miles per hour but eight is a good cadence gait.

Posting Trot

From the slow trot at six miles per hour the rider advances the speed to eight and lets the horse thrust him upward and forward, with the knee angles open and the legs remaining in place. As he comes backward and downward, the knee angle closes.

Remember, let the horse throw you upward and forward and you sink back—not sit down in your saddle.

Reward and Punishment

At this stage of your riding knowledge, you can and should use only the elementary aids which I have described for rewarding or punishing your horse. When your legs close against his sides asking for an increase in speed, consider this a punishment, even though a necessary one. When he has responded by an increase in speed, your hands close on the reins, asking for a decrease and the horse comes down to the slower gait, be quick to relax the pressure against his mouth. Again, this is his reward.

Every time you ride a horse, you are helping either to school or to unschool him. Stay on the horses you can control with ease and security, insist on his obedience to your wishes when you know the horse has understood what it is you are asking of him, and be quick to reward this obedience by relaxing pressure on mouth or sides.

The Canter

A horse should go into a canter from a slow trot. If you are at a posting trot, come back to a slow sitting trot and then, using your legs, put your horse into a canter.

When a horse is cantering, the speed should be between ten and twelve miles per hour and the rider should be in a three-point contact.

Jumping

This first stage of learning to jump is one the beginner may learn at the same time he is learning the posting trot. As I explained back in the chapter on "Position", everything the rider does is fitting him for the jumping, showing, and hunting he will do as soon as his seat in the saddle has become secure and he has learned the meaning and importance of a line of sight. To get and keep a line of sight, the rider should not only have learned

to keep his eyes forward but also to keep them focused on one special point or object. The best way to acquire the habit is for the instructor to stand in front of the jump, reminding the pupil to keep his eyes focused on him, the instructor.

There is no magic formula for learning how to jump and looking well while you are learning. Jumping even the quite high jumps does *not* take special physical attributes, or any exceptional athletic skill or ability. It takes only two things; experience and *knowledge*.

Now that the rider is about to learn how to assume a jumping position and to hold it over his first jump—either a real or imaginary rail on the ground—it is time to realize that all his future work and the rapidity with which progress can be made, depends entirely upon him developing confidence. This can be done by riding the right kind of horse—and learning slowly.

First Stage

1. The rider is trotting around the ring at the slow or six-mile-an-hour trot in a jumping position, maintaining a three-point contact which consists of: the crotch deep in the saddle; the inner bones of the knees and the calves of the legs against the horse's sides; and the upper body inclined forward.

2. Before approaching the jump—which is either a rail on the ground or an *imaginary* rail on the ground—he moves his hands halfway up the horse's crest, preferably using the mane to steady himself.

3. The rider keeps this position, whether the horse actually makes a little hopping jump over the rail on the ground or whether he merely trots over it. It is not an exercise in jumping; it is an exercise in learning to take and to hold the proper jumping position. For this reason, the rider should practice this stage of first grade jumping for quite some time.

From the time the rider is learning to trot over his very first rail on the ground, he must start to learn that all-important and fundamental principle of successful and, therefore, safe jumping: waiting for his horse. The rider takes his position, as described above and holds it, whether the horse jumps or not. He does not anticipate the jump. The rider, in other words, does not "jump" any more than he pulls himself up out of the saddle when he is learning to post.

In posting, the horse throws you up by the thrust of his hindquarters; you sink down, and his forward motion carries you back. In jumping, the upward thrust comes from the horse's forehand, thrusting the rider forward and upward, and he then sinks down in the saddle.

Making a conscious effort to jump when the rider thinks the horse is—or isn't—going to jump, puts the rider *ahead* of his horse, not *with* his horse. When the rider is ahead of the horse, he has lost much of his security and most of his control over his horse.

Obviously, while the rider is in this grade of jumping, his instructor must see to it that he has a horse requiring little or no control, quiet and obedient. The rider must have nothing on his mind but the job of learning to keep his eyes on a point, to move his hands forward, taking his correct jumping position and holding it.

Time spent practicing this exercise on a horse will be time well spent, because the rider who can learn to move his hands forward automatically under any and all jumping conditions, to keep his eyes up and feel what his horse is going to do instead of guessing or anticipating, is on the way to being a rider with a secure seat. It is important at this stage for the rider to keep his hands on the horse's crest and not allow them to move backwards.

3. TAKE-OFF: The rider holds this position; the thrust of the horse throws him forward. The rider doesn't "jump". He waits and as the horse jumps, the rider is thrown forward and upward by the thrust of the horse.

The hip angles close; the knee angles remain open.

2. THE APPROACH: A distance of from five to twenty yards away from the jump. a) Eyes are on a point. b) The hands move halfway up the horse's crest, or mane. The rider places the weight of the upper body on the hands and crest. c) The weight of legs and base goes into the rider's heels and not the stirrups. Contact is maintained through the inner bones of the knees and calves of the legs.

1. In the final stage of first grade jumping, the rider is permitted to canter into a cross-rail. From a slow trot he puts his horse in a canter.

4. **THE FLIGHT:** The rider holds his position. He is now in two-point contact.

5. **THE LANDING:** The hip angles open, knee angles close, the rider starts to sink down—not sit down—in the saddle, the flexed-in ankles and inner bones of knees acting to absorb shock of landing.

6. The rider resumes contact with the horse's mouth and continues the canter in the three-point contact.

The rider's hands are halfway up the horse's crest, the weight of the rider's upper body is on the rider's hands and the horse's crest. The rider maintains a three-point contact. *The weight of the rider's legs and base goes to the rider's depressed heels* and *not to the stirrups.*

In the final stage of first grade jumping, the rider is cantering toward the jump, whereas in the first stage the rider was in a trot going toward the jump. You will find that assuming the jumping position while trotting over a real, or imaginary, rail on the ground creates no nervous strain or tension whatsoever. If the rider is apprehensive about the size jump he is about to take, a good rule of thumb to follow is, he shouldn't be jumping that high! Horses are quick to sense even the slightest hesitancy of the rider, and the horse quickly loses his own heart, or confidence.

The rider is kept at the slow gait, namely the trot, while he begins to accustom his body angles to the slight shock of jumping a cross-rail and getting the actual feel of a jump.

It is absolutely mandatory while the rider is going through these early stages of learning how to jump that he be *mounted on a safe, quiet, steady horse.* The rider should not be asked to think about controlling his horse until some security over even a very low jump has been achieved.

He now begins to get not only the feeling of a jump, but also the feeling of speed going into the jump. The speed, at this stage, is still controlled and should be approximately 10 to 12 miles per hour. Of course, the rider is still on a horse that has to be urged rather than one that has to be held. But he is now asked to put his horse into a canter. Approximately 10 yards away from the jump he releases his horse, holding his position until the horse has cleared the jump.

Exercises: A horse in fair condition can take this cross-rail jump approximately 100 times in an hour.

For the first exercise, the rider concentrates on keeping his eyes on some point directly ahead. The exercise consists of keeping the eyes on that point and then concentrating on keeping the weight of the upper body and the hands on the horse's crest. This is called his release. If instead of pushing, the hands pull, it is wrong. I recommend the use of the mane in these extremely early stages because there is nothing more harmful to both horse and rider than the risk of having the rider's hands come back to interfere with the horse's mouth.

Keep at this exercise until hands push down on the crest for at least ten consecutive jumps.

In the second exercise, the rider concentrates on his heels. The weight of the base and the legs goes into the heels; the foot rests on the stirrup; and as little weight as possible goes into the stirrup. By letting weight sink into the heels you form a vise with your legs, which is the foundation of a sound, secure, educated seat.

Summary and Important Points To Have Mastered

1. Eyes forward—knowing the difference between looking and seeing.
2. Release hands forward on crest—not interfering with horse's mouth.
3. Heels down, contact below knee.

   Be constructive. Never say you or others are doing badly, if you don't really know what it is you, or they, are doing.

For the Aid of Amateur or Professional Teachers

The Five Commandments:

1. Communication—Tell them.
2. Application—They do it.
3. Demonstration—You or your assistant demonstrates lesson.
4. Repeat application—You make them do it.
5. Repetition—Do it over again, again and again.

SECTION TWO

Stable Management

Part I

Grooming	29
Equipment	33

Part II

Cleaning Tack by Robert Freels, Stable Manager, U.S.E.T.	41
Bandaging by Robert Freels	42
Braiding by Robert Freels	44

STABLE MANAGEMENT

PART I

Grooming

A NYONE who owns, or ever hopes to own, a horse may be called upon at some time or another to groom him. It is well to know the safe, proper way to do it. Just as a good cook is able to give constructive criticism to anyone who cooks for him, a rider who really knows how his horse should be turned out, can ask—or even demand—that the groom clean his mount properly.

If you happen to be in charge of your own horse, the first thing to know is how to lead him out of his stall. Many beginners are apprehensive about leading a horse. The safe and proper way to lead a horse is simply to

To Pick Up a Hind Foot

1. Stand well forward of the horse's haunches, facing to the rear. Gently stroke the back as far as the point of the hip against which the inside hand is placed for support.

2. With the outside foot well advanced, stroke the leg down as far as the middle of the cannon with ouside hand. While the inside hand presses the horse's weight over to the opposite hind leg, thus lightening the foot desired to be picked up, grasp the cannon with the outside hand just above the fetlock joint, lift the foot directly toward yourself, so that the leg is bent at the hock.

3. Then move to the rear, keeping the hind leg next to your thigh until his inside foot comes opposite his outside foot. The most common fault is holding the foot out to one side of the horse causing him to resist, due to the discomfort of his position.

1. Stand with the back to the horse's head and place the inside hand on the horse's shoulder.

To Pick Up a Front Foot

2. Bending over, run the outside hand gently but firmly down the back of the leg until the hand is just above the fetlock. Press against the horse's shoulder with the inside hand, thus forcing his weight onto the opposite foreleg.

3. Grasp the tendons just above the fetlock with the fingers and the horse will usually raise his foot. If he does not raise the foot, it can be easily lifted, since all his weight is now carried on the opposite foreleg.

walk forward. The horse will follow. The more you try to stay out of the way of his feet, or look back at him, the more chance you will get stepped on. If the horse is reluctant to move, gently push him off balance to the right, then immediately move out. If you are leading with a halter-shank, grasp the shank about six or eight inches from the snap-hook with the right hand, taking the bight of the shank in the left. Never wrap the bight, or loop of the halter-shank, around the hand or wrist. The horse may bolt or rear causing serious personal injury.

To Clean Out the Feet

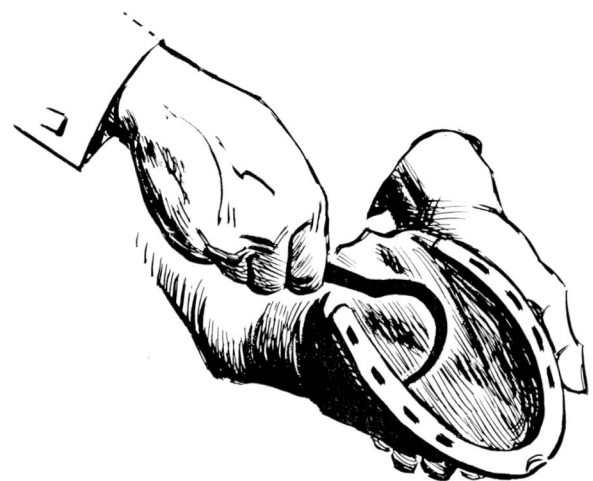

Few things about the care and grooming of a horse are as important as seeing that his feet are properly cleaned. Every rider should know enough about his horse to be able to pick up his horse's feet, before setting out on a ride, to be sure that they are properly cleaned out. Much unsoundness and lameness could be prevented by making use of this simple precaution.

To clean out the feet, always work in order: near fore, near hind, off fore, and off hind. Grasp the hoof pick in the hand opposite the side on which you are working (i.e., if you are on the near side, hold the hoof pick in the right hand, if on the off side, hold it in the left hand). With the hoof pick supported by the heel of the hand, clean out the foot from heel to toe. It is very important that the commissures and the cleft be thoroughly cleaned out, as these places are the seat of thrush. Care should be exercised in cleaning the cleft that it is not deepened by cutting the horn of the frog. Inspect the feet for thrush, torn frog, loose shoes, etc., while cleaning.

Safety Precautions Around Horses

The horse is a timid animal and reacts violently when frightened. However, there is no need to be afraid of horses if certain common-sense precautions are used. The reverse of this is true also; that is, if a rider is overconfident or careless in his actions about horses, sooner or later he will be injured.

Always give warning to a horse when you walk up behind it: The horse is always on the defensive. If it suddenly becomes aware of something in the rear of it, its immediate instinct, prompted by fear, is either to kick or run. If tied, or confined in a stall, the animal cannot run, so it usually kicks. When a rider is kicked it is usually through his own carelessness in not observing this rule. If it is necessary to approach a horse from the rear, speak to it to warn of your presence. As soon as the animal is aware of you, stroke it gently on the croup and move calmly to the head, keeping close to the horse's body.

In any work about a horse, work from a position as near the shoulder as possible: In this way, you cannot be touched by either front or hind feet of the horse.

Always work close to a horse: If this rule is followed, you cannot be struck by the feet, nor will you receive the full force of a kick. This is particularly true when working about the haunches.

Always let the horse know what you intend to do: For instance, when picking up the feet, do not reach for and seize the foot hurriedly. This will startle the horse and may cause him to kick.

Attendants should not be loud or rowdy about horses: This tends to make a horse jumpy and nervous, both on the ground and under saddle. Eventually, some horses will react to this sort of conduct by kicking. A sharp tone of voice may be used for checking an animal, but its loudness should never be any more than required to meet the situation.

Use of Grooming Equipment

The currycomb: The currycomb is used with a light, circular motion. Its primary purpose is to break up caked mud, dried sweat and matted hair. It is *never* used below the knees or on or below the hocks. The horse is very sensitive in these portions due to the bone lying directly under the hide. The above rule will be applied wherever the bone is close to the horse's outer surface, such as the point of the hip, the shoulder, etc. The currycomb should be very carefully used when working about the belly as the skin there is thin and sensitive. The currycomb is also used to clean the brush. The currycomb should be frequently cleaned by rapping the *side* of it smartly against a hard surface several times.

The brush: The brush is the principal tool used in grooming. It should always be held in the hand nearest the horse's head, except when working in difficult spots, such as the inside of the hind legs, down low on the legs, or under the neck. In using the brush, you should stand well away from the animal, keep the arm stiff, and throw the weight of his body against the brush which is applied in straight strokes. In this manner, the bristles of the brush will loosen and remove dirt and scurf from the hide and coat and stimulate circulation. This is the basic function of grooming and is essential to good health and appearance of the horse. The brush is cleaned with the currycomb every two or three strokes, the brush being held *over* the currycomb so that the dirt, when loosened, will fall out of the brush. In brushing the belly, apply the brush the way of the hair.

The grooming cloth: The grooming cloth is used to wipe the eyes, ears, nostrils and dock, also to polish off the horse's coat. In working about the head, the action must be gentle so as not to excite or irritate the horse, particularly if he is head-shy. Care must be used in wiping out the eyes and nostrils in order that these organs will not be injured. In wiping out the dock, the tail should be held about 9 or 10 inches from its root and well elevated with the left hand, using the grooming cloth with the right. Always stand close to and directly in rear of the horse, so that in case the animal kicks, you will not receive the full force of the blow. If the tail is held high and the grooming cloth used gently the horse will not usually object to this operation. When polishing off the coat, apply briskly in the direction in which the hair lies.

Adjustment and Care of Equipment

The rider's comfort and safety will be greatly enhanced by the careful selection of the proper equipment. There are many different types of saddles, and some riders—particularly hunting people—scorn the forward seat, or jumping saddle, while others feel that there's no saddle on earth to be compared with a good, deep, well broken-in Pariani. I must confess that a Pariani is my own choice for a jumping saddle. But the important thing is to choose a saddle in which the rider sits comfortably, and one that's well treed and padded so that there is no friction against the horse's back. As a rule, economy in the purchase of equipment is extravagance. The veterinary bills for a horse's sore back will come to a great deal more than the price of a good saddle!

The controversies among grooms, riders and professional horsemen regarding the relative merits of the different types of bits and martingales are endless and never-ending. The bit should fit the horse—both physically and temperamentally. The only proper bit for your horse is the bit which he accepts willingly, goes in quietly, and to which he responds readily.

If you have a horse with a difficult, a bad, or a dead mouth, a good idea is to change the bitting fairly frequently. A Pelham and Curb chain act on the bars of the horse's mouth, a snaffle works on the cheeks. Therefore, if you switch back and forth, using a bit of equal severity, but one that reacts on a different part of your horse's mouth, you will generally find the horse responding more easily.

A few general suggestions about equipment: When showing a hunter in a hack class, it is preferable to use a double bridle or Pelham. A great many hunter judges will simply refuse to pin a hunter that is shown in a snaffle or single rein bridle. It is against A.H.S.A. rules to use a martingale.

All leather should be kept soft and pliable, both for the preservation of the leather and its appearance. It is difficult for a rider to close his hands on the reins, if they are stiffened and thickened with dirt. Bits and stirrup irons should be polished regularly.

Some bits are more severe than others, but all bits become severe in the hands of the rider who is so insecure or so uncertain that he is constantly going to his reins for support, therefore constantly abusing his horse's mouth. For this reason, never use more bit than you need for controlling the horse.

General Notes on the Use of the Curb Bit

The curb bit is effective through *leverage* rather than pressure. The extent of its severity depends upon the length of the shank: the longer the shank, the more severe the bit. As hunters should not be over-flexed, care should be taken to avoid over-bitting that can cause the horse to become over-flexed and fretful.

The curb bit should be a quarter of an inch below the snaffle and must be wide enough to avoid pinching the horse's lips. The curb chain should be twisted until flat, then fitted into the groove in the horse's lower lip. It should be loose enough for the shank to form an angle of forty-five degrees with the horse's lower jaw when tension is applied to the rein. A leather lip strap keeps the bit and chain in place. The chain should pass below the snaffle.

The effect of the curb bit is to draw the chin in and bring the head down.

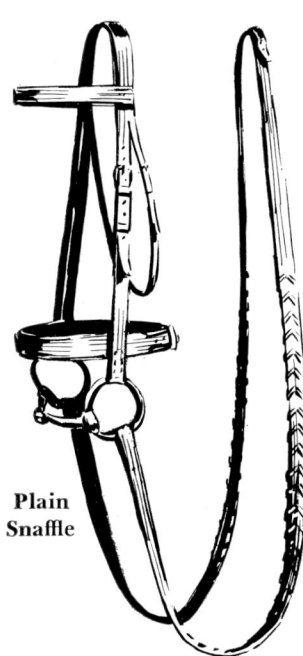

Plain Snaffle

This is the mildest of all bits, acting mainly on the cheeks. It is the least harmful bit, even in the hands of the most inexperienced rider. Its main effect is to raise the horse's head. When adjusting the plain snaffle, fit it snugly into the corners of the horse's mouth. It is correctly adjusted when you have a single wrinkle at the corners of the horse's mouth.

Halter

When a halter is properly adjusted, the crownpiece passes just in the rear of the ears and will remain in that position without slipping. The noseband is in a position on the face two inches below the points of the cheek-bones. The most frequent fault is a position too low. It is important that the loose end of the crownpiece be passed through the buckle and ring as given above, as any loose end of that sort sticking out is liable to be seized by another horse in his teeth. This is the way many halters are broken!

The Pelham bit is similar to the curb but limits the use of the latter because a snaffle ring is attached to the upper part of the branch of the bit, either loosely or as an integral part of the bit. Pelham bits vary in severity according to the length of the shank (which should not exceed 4 inches for a hunter) and the tension of the curb chain. Obviously, the shorter shank lessens the leverage and force of the curb, therefore the shortest possible shank should be used.

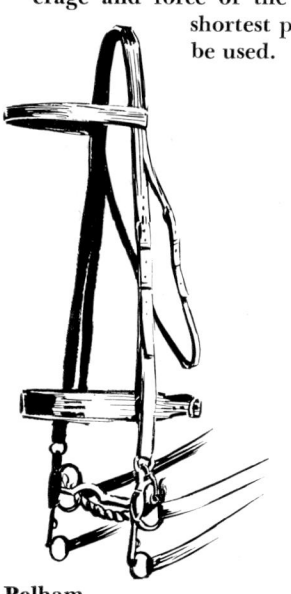

Pelham

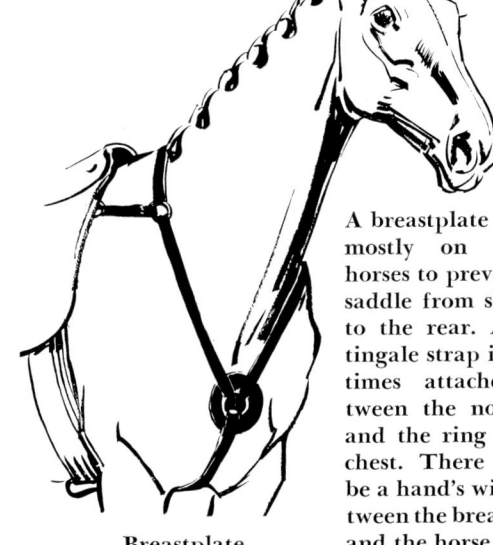

Breastplate

A breastplate is used mostly on slender horses to prevent the saddle from slipping to the rear. A martingale strap is sometimes attached between the noseband and the ring on the chest. There should be a hand's width between the breastplate and the horse.

The Wire Snaffle

The wire snaffle is made effective by the same principle as the plain snaffle. Its use is advisable where the plain snaffle is not strong enough. Many people feel that the wire snaffle is an unusually severe bit, but I can only say that the severity of any bit in a horse's mouth is in direct proportion to the skill and steadiness of a rider's hands.

A Double Bridle,

or Snaffle-and-Curb,

or Bit-and-Bridoon

This is a double bridle, also known as a bit-and-bridoon, also known as a snaffle-and-curb. It is used most commonly as a bridle because it has both a snaffle and a curb, so adjusted that they may be used either individually or together, depending upon the effect to be achieved.

Bridling the Horse

Take the reins in right hand, crownpiece in left hand. Approach the horse on left side, passing right hand along his neck. Slip reins over horse's head and let them rest on his neck. Remove halter. Take crownpiece in right hand and snaffle bit in left hand. Bring crownpiece in front of and slightly below proper position. Insert left thumb into side of horse's mouth above tusk and press upon lower jaw causing him to open his mouth. Insert bit by raising crownpiece and, with right hand, quietly draw the ears under crownpiece. Secure throatlatch.

The bridle should be adjusted so that the snaffle bit will touch lightly the upper corners of the lips and so that the throatlatch will admit four finger-breadths between it and the throat.

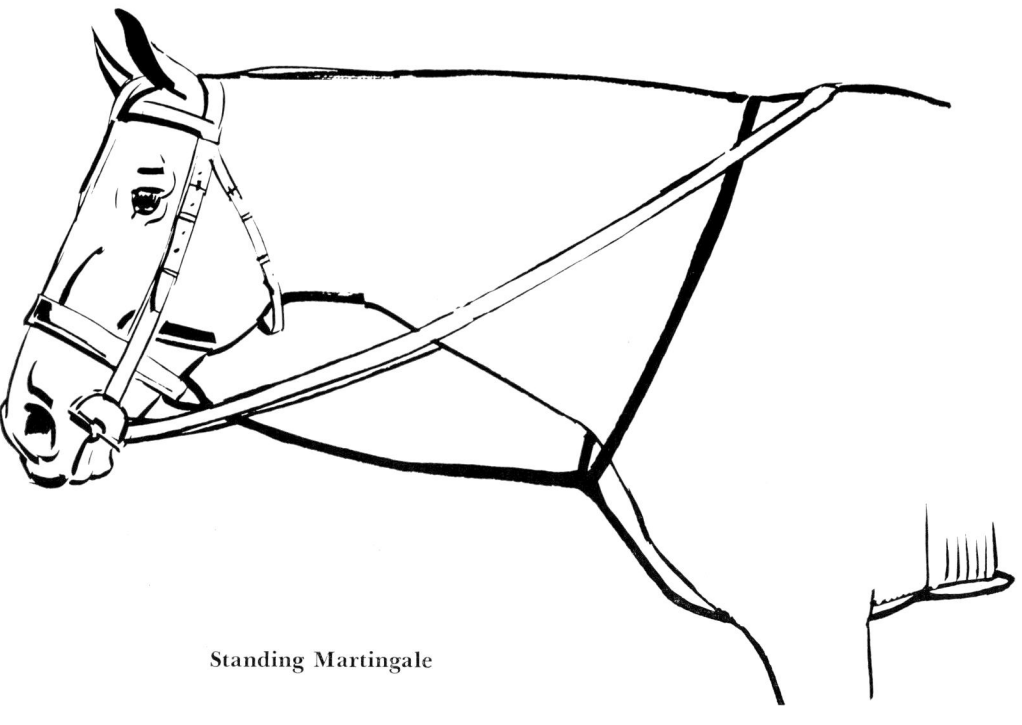

Standing Martingale

A Standing Martingale

The standing martingale is used primarily to prevent excessively high head carriage which makes the proper effects of the bit impossible. Slow motion films give evidence that the standing martingale does not at any time interfere with the jumping horse if it is not too tight. It may, therefore, be used as often as necessary.

The Running Martingale

The running martingale is preferred by some because it helps to lower the horse's head through pressure on the bit; viz.: the usual effect of a snaffle bit in a horse's mouth is on the cheeks. When a running martingale is used, and adjusted correctly, the pressure of the snaffle is transferred to the bars. Any pressure on the bars, brings the horse's chin in, relaxes his jaw, and so tends to lower the head carriage. For this reason, the running martingale can be used with great success by the experienced rider. But the dangers are obvious,—the running martingale applies constant pressure on the bars of the horse's mouth and can soon produce a bad-mouthed horse.

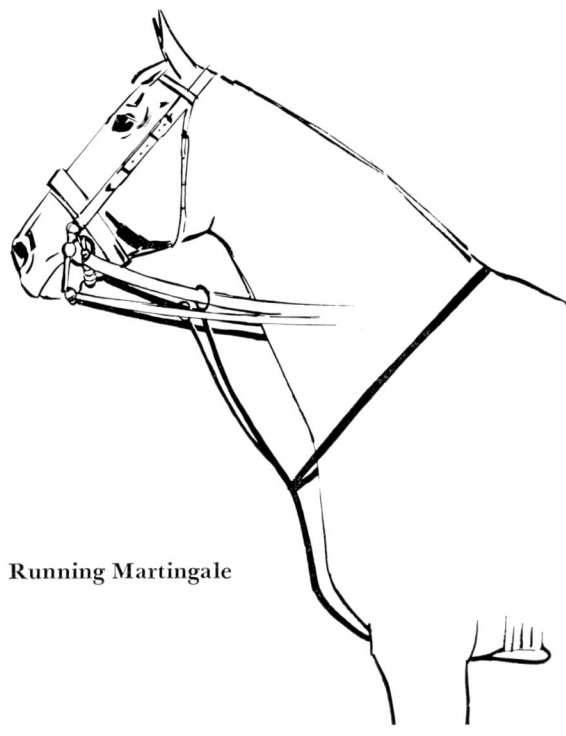

Running Martingale

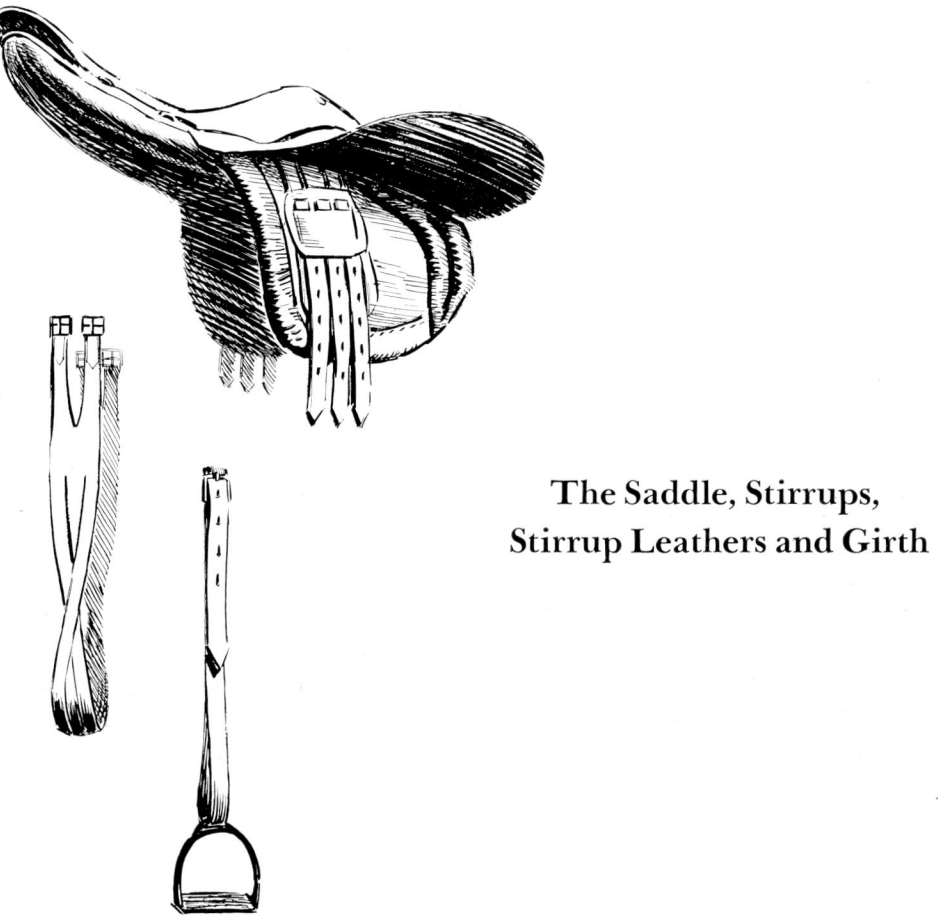

The Saddle, Stirrups, Stirrup Leathers and Girth

Adjustment of the Saddle

After the saddle has been placed on the horse's back and prior to letting down the girth, grasp the saddle by the pommel and lightly shake it from left to right three or four times. This will settle the saddle in its proper position on the horse and will practically eliminate the possibility of pinched withers due to having the saddle too far in the front.

Adjustment of the Girth

When the girth has been secured, the horse's forelegs should be picked up—first the near and then the off—and gently pulled to the front as far as possible. This insures a smooth lay of the hair and hide under the girth, and will, to a great extent, prevent girth sores. When tightened, the rider should be able to place two fingers between the horse and the girth. This is the correct adjustment.

This is a Hitchcock Girth, good for horses susceptible to girth sores.

Budd

PART II

Cleaning Tack

By ROBERT FREELS, Stable Manager, U.S.E.T.

CLEAN tack not only is necessary for appearance's sake, but also for the health of your horse. Dirty saddles are the cause of many irritations leading to sore backs and girth galls. For your convenience, you should invest in a cleaning hook and a saddle rack.

Before applying any man-made product to your leather, it must be thoroughly cleaned with a sponge soaked in warm water. In order to get every corner clean, it is necessary to unbuckle all of your various pieces especially in a bridle.

After all remains of sweat and mud are removed, use a clean, small sponge to apply glycerine saddle soap. Be careful to use very little water, as you don't want to create suds. Rub in thoroughly.

The metal parts of your tack, stirrups, buckles, and the bit, should be wiped with a metal polish of your choice. A soft rag will add a shiny finishing touch to your efforts.

If you get caught out riding in the rain and your tack gets a good soaking, apply Neatsfoot Oil to soften and restore it to its previous softness.

Bandaging

There are many different types of bandages of which everyone should have some knowledge. I will explain some of the types and when to use them.

A. Antiphlogistine Poultice Bandage

Let us imagine your horse has received a blow while jumping, and you suspect there will be a swelling in the injured area. You should heat whatever type of poultice you are using to a temperature just hot enough to still be handled. The other materials you will need are: one flannel bandage, eight sheets of cotton, and a roll of wax paper or oiled silk to insulate the leg. Apply the poultice over the bruised area. By dipping your hand in warm water, you can mold the poultice without having it stick to your hand. The poultice should be one-half to three-quarters of an inch thick when the application is finished. Now you are ready to wrap the wax paper tightly around the leg covering the afflicted area. This keeps the head in the poultice.

You are then ready to wrap your sheet cotton on the leg in a neat manner. Always remember to wrap the cotton and bandage to the rear of your horse so that the pressure you pull on the bandage is on the cannon bone and not on the tendon. Take your flannel bandage and wrap it tight enough to keep the cotton snug to the leg. To finish, pin the end of the bandage on the outside of the leg or hold it in place by wrapping tape around the end. Either method is practical and safe.

B. Knee and Hock Bandages

Your horse may injure his knee or hock and you will run into difficulty getting it bandaged. The best solution to your problem is called a "Spider Bandage." First you need a piece of strong material about the size of a feed sack. Cut in eight inches toward center from both sides, making approximately 15 one-inch strips down each side. Apply your poultice to the joint and cover with wax paper. You are now ready to use your sheet cotton; two rolls sometimes being necessary to cover an area large enough so that the bandage stays secure. Now wrap one flannel bandage above the knee or hock and one below, but never actually bandage with pressure over the joint. You can now use the "spider bandage" you have made. Place it around the leg starting at the top of the cotton. Pull the top two strings around the leg and twist together in a half of a square knot. Tuck the ends down and reach around for the second two, doing the same with the extra ends. Continue until the entire leg is done. Always remember to tie the knots behind the joint, behind the knee and in front of the hock.

C. White Lotion Bandage

White lotion is a cooling lotion made by crushing about 4 to 6 tablets in one gallon of water. Anytime your horse has heat or swelling around the ankle or tendon, your best remedy is to use this lotion. Begin by taking 6 or 7 sheets of cotton and soaking them thoroughly in the solution. Wrap these around the leg, starting higher than usual since the wet bandage will slip down on the leg. You are now ready for the flannel bandage, which is put on the same as before. Be careful not to bandage too tightly around the top, as you will want to be able to pour some more of your white lotion inside the bandage. It is a good idea to wet the outside of the bandage, too. If you apply white lotion on the inside only, it will form an insulation and keep in the heat you are trying to get out.

D. Rest Bandages

Rest bandages are used after a hard workout such as a strenuous hunt or a busy day of showing.

First you need some good leg brace or liniment such as Absorbine, Dixie Rub or Limber Leg. You should apply the brace to the tendons and ankles and rub until the leg is fairly dry. Then apply your cotton, and here I would suggest seven or eight sheets to assure your horse the most comfort. Cover with a flannel bandage, starting one-quarter of the way from the top and working down, making it hold snugly. When you are below the ankle start back up. This gives the leg two layers over the most vital point of his leg. Upon reaching the top, fold whatever bandage is left so that the end finishes on the outside of the leg. This gives the horse no chance of pulling it loose by catching it with his opposite hoof. These bandages should be left on no longer than overnight.

E. Sweat Bandages

Sweat bandages are applied to injuries where all the heat is gone, but where there still remains a swelling or enlargement.

Freely apply a sweat lotion to the leg and rub for two minutes. Insert some oiled silk or wax paper in the center of your sheet cotton to act as insulation. This allows the cotton next to the leg to absorb some of the sweat that will be created. The cotton will be very soiled when you remove it the next day, but you should reuse it as long as possible as the excess sweat helps reduce your problem leg. Finish by wrapping the flannel bandage in the same manner as the rest bandage.

Braiding

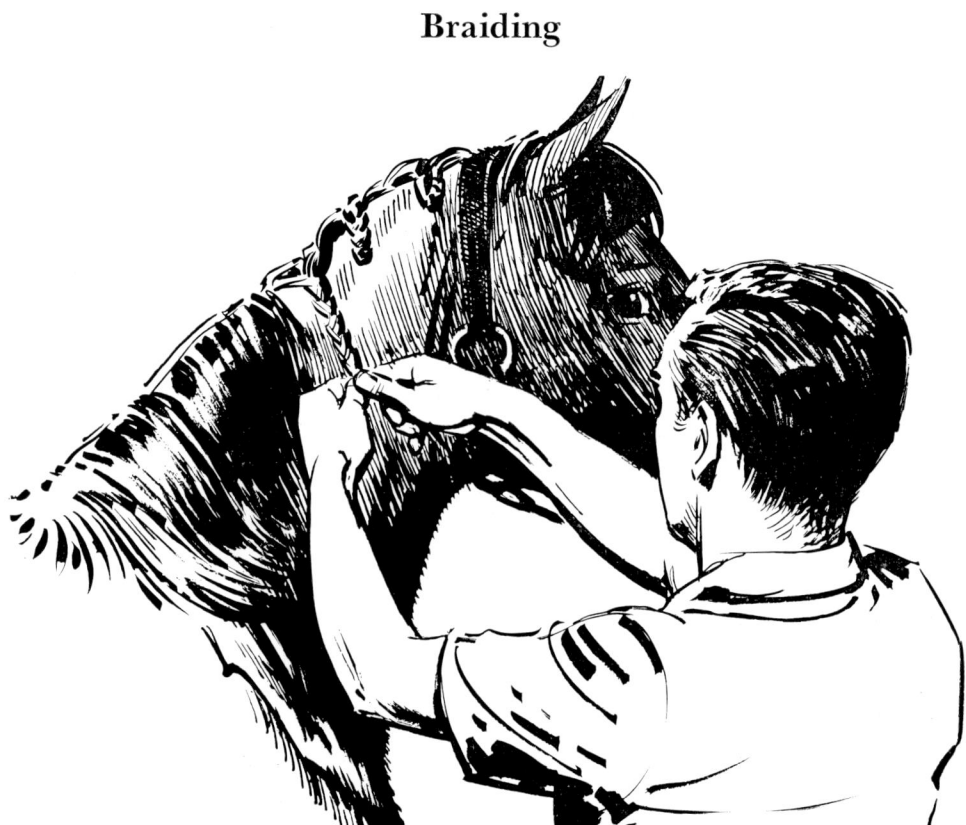

Braiding your horse's mane and tail for a show or a day's hunting is similar to shining your shoes or wearing a white shirt and tie. If you wish to make a neat appearance, always braid for a special occasion. It is certain to improve the looks of your horse. If he has a short neck, have numerous, small braids to give the impression his neck is longer than it actually is. Conversely, a long-necked horse should have fewer, thicker braids. Braiding the tail improves the appearance of the hind quarters. A horse that is narrow through the quarters or has blemished hocks can be helped by braiding with bigger strands and by not going too far down the tailbone. If your horse's quarters are big and coarse, fine them out by small strands and by braiding to the very end of his tailbone.

To braid the mane, you should first be certain that it is clean and thoroughly combed. It should be pulled to five or six inches in length. You will need a mane comb for this, and it is also convenient for measuring the amount of hair to be put in each braid. The comb is about three inches long so take almost the comb's length of hair starting just behind the ears. Divide that into three parts and braid the same as you would a small girl's pigtail. There are several ways of folding the finished braid up to make a loop. The neatest and most secure way is to sew it with a heavy thread and needle. Yarn and rubber bands are also used to hold the looped braid in place, but you will find these are not as neat or secure. When folding them up, keep them even in length and neatly fastened. When the mane is completed, don't forget to do the foretop in the same manner.

Braiding the tail is difficult and takes hours of practice before you can do it properly. The method is called "French Braiding." Start at the top of the tail by taking two small strands of hair—25-30 hairs in each strand—and cross them. Hold these with one hand while you add another strand from the left side. Now you have three strands of hair needed for braiding. Each time you twist the braid you should add another strand to the middle part of the three sections. Be careful not to get too much hair when you add or you will have too large a braid by the time you reach the end of the tailbone. Upon reaching the end or at whatever point you've chosen to end, braid out the three strands you are holding. When finished you can loop it up, sewing each circle of the roll to the previous one.

Robert E. Meeks

SECTION THREE

The Rider—Second Grade

Part I

Reins	49
Aids	51
The Posting Trot	53
Turns	59
Schooling	62
Jumping	70
Showing the Hunter	72

Part II

Longeing by Bertalan de Nemethy, Coach, U.S.E.T.	73

Part III

Fox Hunting by Mrs. John J. McDonald, Ex-MFH, Meadowbrook Hunt	80

THE RIDER—SECOND GRADE

PART I

Reins

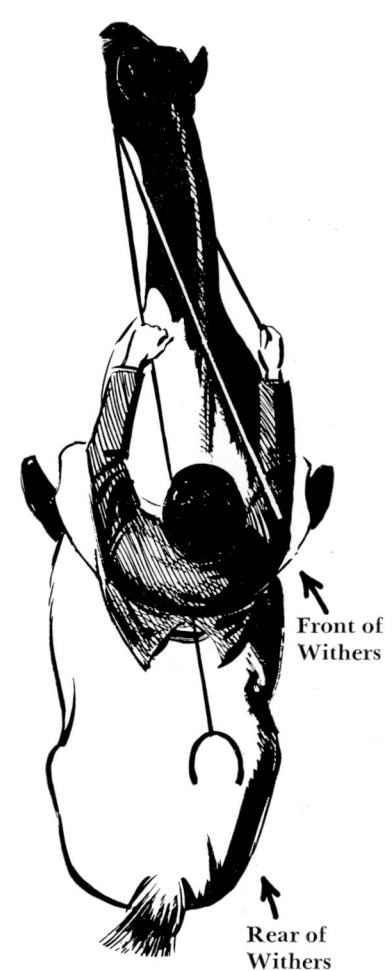

The Indirect Reins

A. *The indirect rein in front of the withers* forms a line from horse's mouth through horse's withers and displaces the weight of the horse's forehand from one shoulder to the other.

B. *The indirect rein in rear of the horse's withers* forms a line from horse's mouth to point of hip, displaces the weight from one shoulder to the other and to his hind quarter on the same side as the displaced shoulder.

C. *The Pulley Rein.* This is a very strong rein. It works like a pulley and displaces the horse's weight from forehand to hind quarters. It works as a  very good emergency brake when a fast stop is necessary. It can also be used to keep a horse straight going around turns. It uses only one side of his mouth. This gives the rider the advantage of having a fresh side to work on, especially when he has an extremely strong going horse in the hunting field. Applications—Either the right or left hand is set or fixed on the horse's withers, while the opposite hand or arm adds pressure to the horse's mouth.

D. *Draw Reins, Pulley effect.* Old horses that don't flex. Odd-mouthed horses. Star gazer—will draw head down.

E. *Drop Noseband.* Is used to keep a horse's mouth closed.

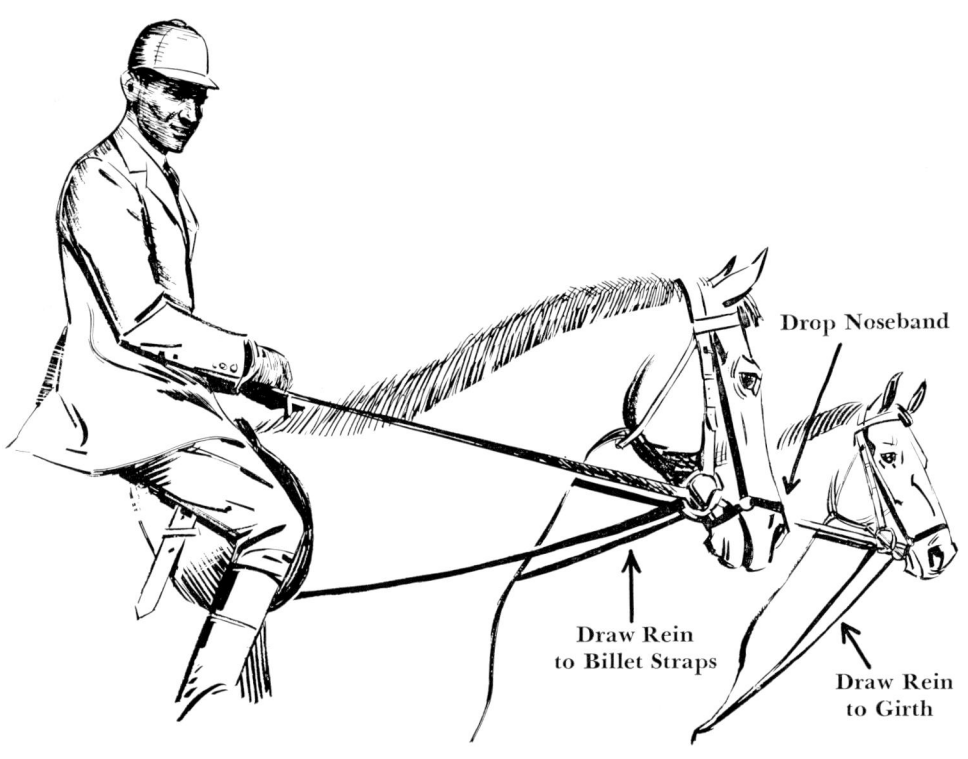

Drop Noseband

Draw Rein to Billet Straps

Draw Rein to Girth

Aids

In an earlier chapter, you learned about the elementary aids and how they work on a horse: primarily the control of the increase and decrease of forward motion. But before going on to the more advanced phases of jumping and riding, the rider should be able to understand and to apply some of the more advanced aids. It should always be remembered that whether we are discussing the use of the aids or controls, in their most elementary or advanced form (which you will come to later in this book), we are always using the same aids, although in different and more complicated ways.

There are two kinds of aids—natural and artificial. The natural aids are the hands, the legs, the weight, the voice. The artificial aids are the spur, the whip or riding bat, numerous types of bits.

Natural Aids

Hands. Active hands apply pressure to the horse's mouth.

Passive hands are in contact with the horse's mouth adding no pressure. A set hand can be either hand taking a feel of the horse's mouth with no give.

Good or educated hands are a combination of active and passive—knowing when to use either one at the correct time. For an increase in speed, the hands must relax before the legs become active. For a decrease in speed, the hands become active and leg pressure is relaxed. For a turn to the right, the right hand is active with the left hand remaining passive. The opposite is true for a left turn.

Legs. Active legs apply pressure to the side of the horse.

Passive legs are in contact with the horse with no pressure. Good or educated legs are also a combination of active and passive, knowing which to use at the correct time. For an increase in speed, the legs become active as the hands relax and vice versa. The rider's outside leg is that on the outer part of a turn or partial turn. The inside leg is that on the inside of a turn or partial turn. When a movement calls for the use of only one leg at a time, care must be exercised, that the opposite leg remain passive.

Weight. The eyes, to a great extent, influence and direct the balance of the upper body in the saddle, so that the rider's weight, as an aid, may be counted on to work automatically as a balance if his eyes are up and correctly focused in the direction in which he intends to go.

Voice. "Whoa!" for decreasing the gait, at first used in accord with reins. "Cluck" for jumping, used in accord with riding bat or spurs.

Before any of these aids can be applied effectively, the horse must be put on the bit. To do this, the rider picks up his reins and establishes contact with his horse's mouth. With the aid of leg pressure the horse in a very simple way has been put "on the bit." The feel of the horse's mouth is light at the slow gaits and becomes stronger as the gaits increase. It is this feel of the bit on the part of the horse that makes it possible for the rider to increase and decrease the horse's speed with a minimum of effort. A horse is said to be "nicely on the bit," when he flexes his jaw and then his poll and accepts a steady feel of his mouth.

A horse who is behind the bit, or one who refuses to accept the bit, is a difficult horse to ride and a tricky horse to jump. A horse signals his intention of running out by dropping behind the bit. The horse who is "behind the bit" can do as he pleases—the horse who is "on the bit" is under control. This controlled horse, on the bit, is the result of a coordination of aids with one following and assisting the other. However, it is extremely important for the rider to remember that the aids are signals to the horse and sometimes very strong signals. They should be used one at a time, although they may and sometimes should follow each other very closely.

Lateral and Diagonal Application of Aids

Lateral application of aids means using rein and leg aids on the same side of the horse. Diagonal application means using rein and leg aids on opposite sides of the horse. Laterals and diagonals will be used in the explanations of the canter and the turns on haunches and forehand.

Voice

The voice can be used effectively to help decrease speed, if at the same time he applies pressure on the reins, the rider uses his voice to say "whoa." The horse will gradually learn to respond to the voice with very little or no pressure on the reins. For those of you who expect to spend much time in the hunting field, this is an especially good exercise. Its rewards will more than repay your patience.

In forward motion, I recommend the use of the voice only when going into a jump. *Exercise:* To produce impulsion, at this time the rider should hold his horse at a standstill, striking him lightly on the flank with a bat and clucking simultaneously. The horse will associate the sound of the voice with the bat, and the rider, one or two strides before the obstacle, will have only to cluck and the horse will respond—you will have the same result as when using a bat.

Artificial Aids

The Spur. The spur should be used when natural leg pressure has failed to produce necessary impulsion.

The Whip or Riding Bat. When natural leg pressure aided by the spur does not produce desired results, then the riding bat should be used. To use it correctly, one should make a bridge of the reins, with the bight on the opposite side of the whip, the hand with the bat comes free of the reins and touches the horse lightly on the flank. The rider's hand returns immediately to his reins. In using the bat, the arm should pivot from the shoulder while the rest of the body stays in position.

Bits. A snaffle bit is inclined to raise a horse's head. A curb bit will bring his chin in and his head down. Bitting a horse has a great deal to do with the conformation and disposition of the horse.

Backing—You can back your horse in two ways:

No. 1. Having your horse on the bit, close your hands so you displace weight from forehand to quarters, then wait for your horse to answer your signal.

No. 2. Having your horse on the bit, close your legs on the horse, the active leg drives your horse into the bit and he comes back off the bit. At first, never try to back more than three steps at a time.

The Posting Trot—There are three ways of posting to the trot: ahead of the motion of your horse, with the motion, and behind the motion. The two correct ways are with and behind the motion.

When I ask the rider to be with the motion of his horse, I mean that his upper body is to be inclined forward over his base so he can adjust the forward inclination of his upper body to the horse's trot. The degree to which the horse thrusts the rider upward and forward is the degree to which the rider's forward inclination of his upper body must be adjusted. One of the most important reasons for teaching this method of posting to the trot is that the pupil who is learning to post with the motion of his horse is, at the same time, learning a correct *jumping* position. Another advantage of posting with the motion—especially for long rides or hunting—is the fact that much of the rider's weight is taken off the horse's back, giving the horse greater freedom of movement and making his work easier.

Posting with the motion also helps to overcome a common tendency of getting the legs too far in front of the girth. When the rider's legs are too far in front of the girth, it is impossible for him to post with the motion. Learning to post with the motion brings the rider's legs into position slightly behind the girth, where they not only contribute to the rider's security, but are in position to become active when necessary. Because it is so difficult for the beginner to learn and to keep the correct degree of forward inclination of the upper body, we often see him tending to get ahead of his horse, or ahead of the motion. This happens when a rider gets out of the saddle too high and transfers his weight ahead of his points of support. Because he is out of balance, as the horse begins to move forward, he is thrown even farther forward so that he collapses on the horse's neck. This tendency on the part of the beginner to anticipate or to get ahead of his horse can be overcome by *learning to wait for his horse*. General Mariles, head of the famous Mexican Army Team, when approached by an admirer and asked for the secret of his incredibly smooth performances over fences, said, "with a horse—*wait!*" *Feel* what your horse is going to do, and then—wait for him. Remember, it is the horse's job to throw you forward and upward. All *you* do is sink down in the saddle.

Posting behind the motion, which should never be confused with posting behind the horse, is not only correct, but also sometimes essential to efficient schooling, when working with green horses, when working to put a horse on the bit, and when working with bold horses.

To Summarize: a. Posting with the motion puts the pupil into the correct jumping position. Posting behind the motion gives more control.

b. It teaches the rider about opening and closing the knee angles that are so important to a smooth performance.

c. It enables all riders of all degrees of skill, to look well on a horse and still feel secure.

Exercise for Posting with the Motion: First *walk*, with the body inclined forward in posting position. Then put the horse into a slow or sitting trot at six miles an hour. *Do not post.* As the horse trots, the rider should feel the crotch—and not the buttocks—hitting the saddle. Now—gradually—let the horse thrust you *forward* and slightly *upward,* then you sink downward and the impulsion of the horse carries you back. In rising to the trot, the angle at the hips should be opened as little as necessary. If the buttocks are in the saddle, you will find that your horse is throwing you upward and forward instead of forward and upward, and you will then be posting *behind* the motion.

The rider should repeat this exercise for five minutes every time he rides.

Diagonals—If the rider is down in the saddle when the right forefoot strikes the ground, he is posting on the right diagonal; if he is down when the left forefoot is planted, he is posting on the left diagonal. The rider should frequently alternate diagonals in order to insure equal development and power in the hind legs of the horse. On straight lines it is immaterial which diagonal the rider posts on, provided he uses both diagonals equally. But when working in a riding hall, a horse travels a great deal of the time on a curve and his outside hind leg travels further than his inside leg. In the ring, on the left hand, for example, the rider should post on the right diagonal, receiving the thrust of the left hind leg, which has the shorter distance to travel, and thus equalizing the work of the hind legs. The opposite, of course, is true when working on the right hand.

A quick and easy way to tell whether or not you are posting on the proper diagonal is to look down at your horse's shoulder. If you are in the saddle when your horse's right shoulder comes toward you, you are on the right diagonal. If the right shoulder is going away from you, you are on the left diagonal.

The Canter

When putting a horse into a canter, the diagonal aids are used. For the right lead, the rider applies the right indirect rein in front of the withers, displacing the weight from the right shoulder to the left, leaving the horse's right foreleg free to move. Then the rider displaces the horse's haunches with his left leg, transferring the horse's weight from the left hind to the right hind. The rider's left leg becomes slightly more active to produce the extra impulsion that puts the horse into a canter.

If a horse has acquired the unfortunate habit of cross-cantering, try cantering him in small circles. The minute you feel him cross-cantering, circle him and keep him at the small circle until he has corrected himself. Then take him back out on the track, repeating the circle again the minute you feel his hind-quarters changing leads. This is no sure cure for this annoying habit, but it sometimes produces results, especially if the rider is also careful to put the horse onto his lead from the slow or sitting trot, collecting him first, making sure the weight is transferred from forehand to hindquarters and kept there.

The Gallop

Two-point and Three-point Contact

When the horse is cantering the rider should have a three-point contact. When the horse is galloping the rider should have a two-point contact. The rider has a three-point contact when his crotch is deep in the saddle and the inner bones of the knees and the calves of the legs are all in contact with the horse.

The rider has a two-point contact when the inner bones of the knees and the calves of the legs are in contact with the saddle and the crotch is out of the saddle. The rider's weight is carried in his heels and this combination of legs and heels forms a vise-like grip on the horse which provides security for the rider even though he is out of the saddle. At the canter, the horse moves at ten to twelve miles an hour; at the hand gallop, fourteen to sixteen miles an hour; and at the extended gallop, eighteen to twenty miles an hour.

As we have seen in a previous chapter, the horse moves at four miles an hour at the walk; six miles an hour at the slow trot; and eight miles an hour at the posting trot.

When jumping, the horse may be expected to jump a three-foot fence safely and well when he is going ten to twelve miles an hour; a three-foot six at twelve to fourteen miles an hour; a four-foot at fourteen to sixteen miles an hour. Very few horses jump safely when going faster than sixteen miles an hour.

The Shoulder-In

. . . is a suppling exercise used for bending and flexing a horse. To do a shoulder-in lateral aids are used. For a right shoulder-in, a right indirect rein and right leg are applied. If the movement is correct, the horse's right hindfoot tracks in approximately the same place as the horse's left forefoot. The opposite aids are used for a left shoulder-in.

Right Indirect Rein
Active Leg

How to Turn or "Bend" Your Horse

1. The rider is looking into the corner and riding with a direct rein.
2. The rider is looking in the opposite corner and applying an indirect rein in front of the withers.
3. At the turn, the rider applies an active inside leg to make the horse bend in the corner, fitting into the corner like a bow.

In the last two movements the rider's eyes are focused on the opposite corner.

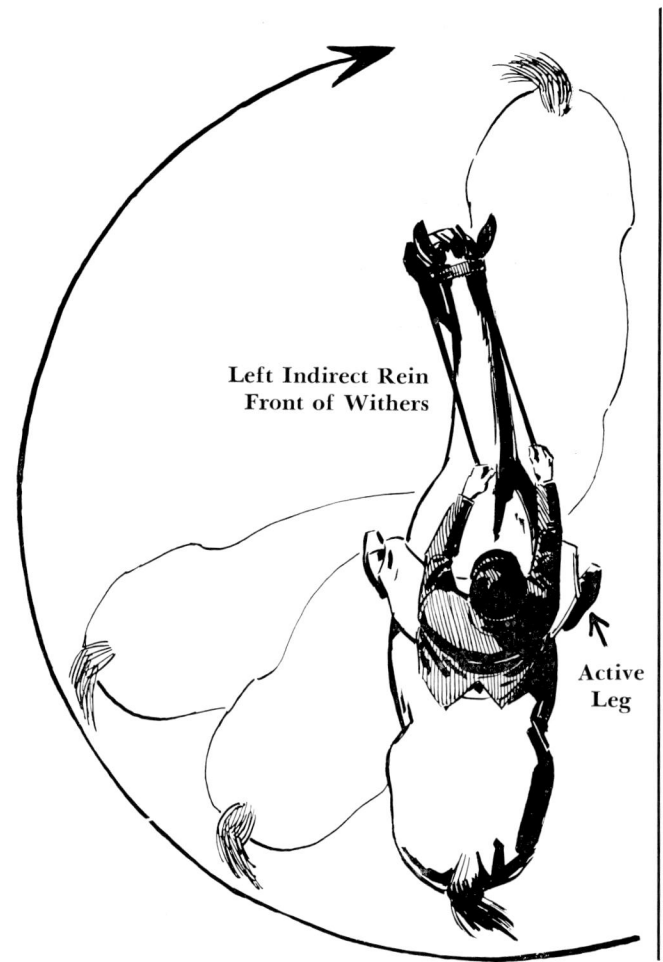

This Is a Turn on the Forehand

Use of Diagonal Aids

1. The direct rein and active legs put the horse on the bit.
2. The left indirect rein in front of the withers displaces the weight from the left fore to the right fore, by forcing that to become the pivot for the turn.
3. An active leg turns the horse, displacing the haunches from right to left.
4. The passive leg becomes active if the horse attempts to back up from the rein action.

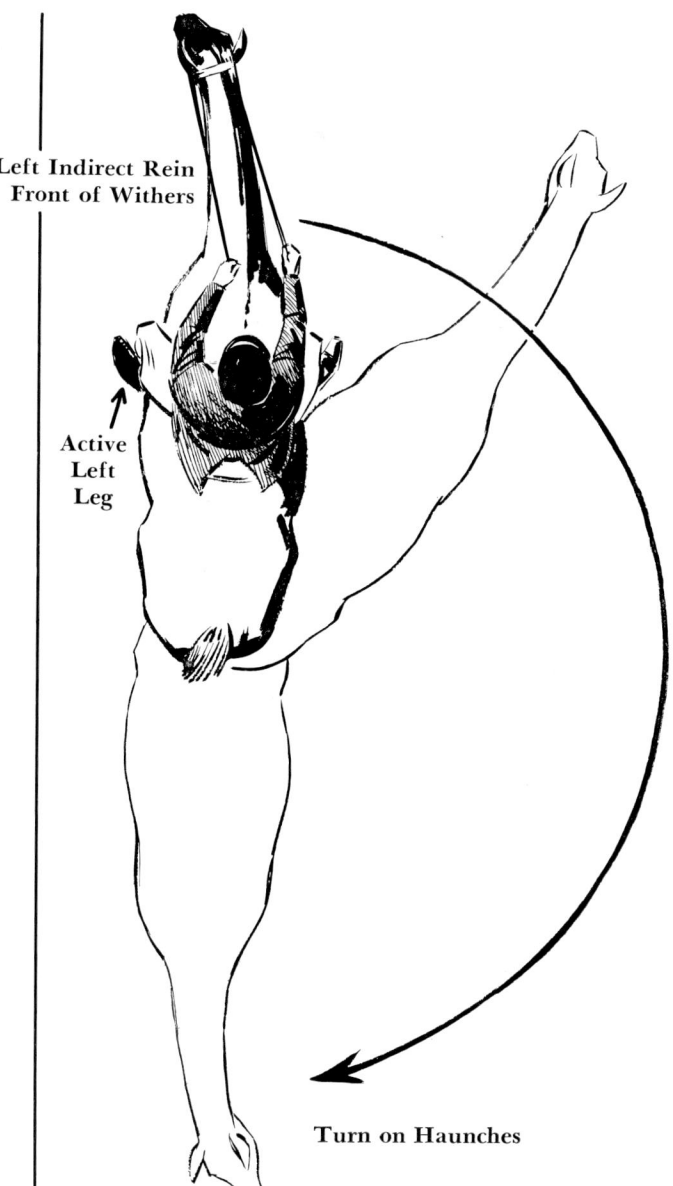

This Is a Turn on the Haunches

Use of Lateral Aids

    A. To train horses and riders.

1. The direct rein and active legs put the horse on the bit.
2. The left indirect rein in front of the withers works together with an active leg.
3. The right direct rein and the right passive leg assist the left indirect rein and the left active leg to make the turn on the haunches.
4. The right passive leg becomes active only if the horse attempts to back up from the rein action.

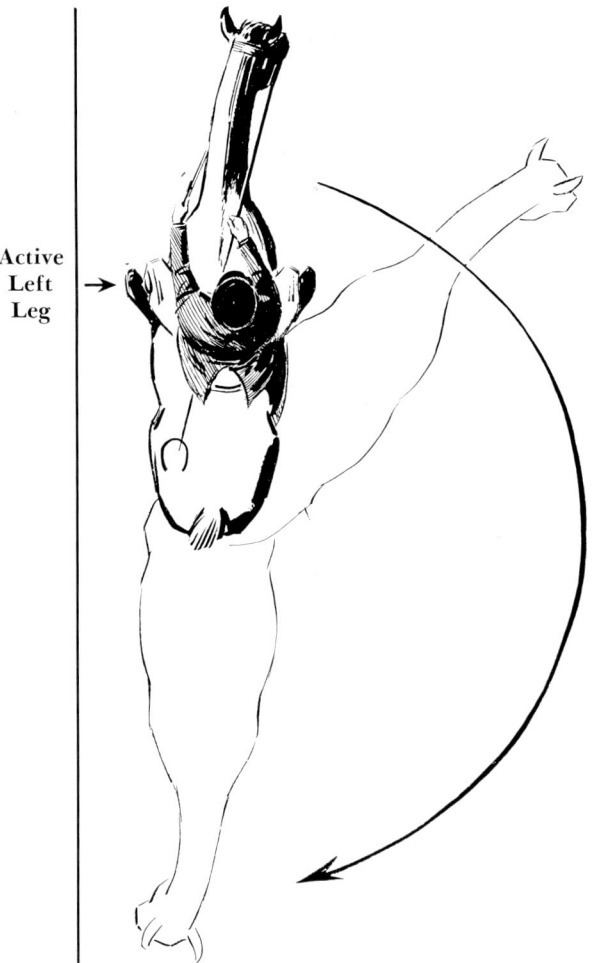

B. After you have learned "A", you apply the diagonal aids for "B" (illus. above). The right indirect rein in rear of withers displaces the weight from right to left shoulder and left haunch, leaving the right foreleg free to move. The rider's left leg becomes active. This keeps the haunches from moving in or back, and with the aid of left passive rein, makes the turn on the haunches.

Schooling

Schooling movements are limbering exercises for your horse. They are important to him, and he should do them fairly regularly for the same reason that human beings should have regular exercise; they keep him fit and in condition.

Schooling movements serve another important purpose: They act as a constant reminder and refresher-course in the use, application and coordination of the aids.

To be effective, any schooling movement that is used should be one that utilizes a horse's shoulder and neck muscles. Schooling movements should also be planned so that they teach the horse responsiveness to the rein and leg aids, and instill in him the habit of obedience to the rider's commands. The following schooling movements call for the use of the different aids, applied either individually, in sequence, or simultaneously. Any, or all of them, are fine exercises for both horse and rider, particularly when working in the ring and limbering up before taking a course of jumps. It is never a good idea just to work a horse around in a circle. He should be kept limber and alert by asking him to perform such simple exercises as these, which will help make and keep him a better athlete, and, therefore, a better jumper.

Recommended Schooling Movements

Trotting and Stopping

This is an excellent exercise to teach the rider coordination of the aids in stopping his horse, and to help "mouth" a young, green, or badly-mouthed horse. Trot a third of the way around the ring, then apply a direct rein aid, keeping eyes up, and closing hands on reins, apply and hold pressure until the horse comes to a standstill. Relax hands for reward. Keep the horse at the standstill to the count of five, then put the horse into forward motion once more, from the walk to the slow trot to the posting trot. Another third of the way around the ring, the hands again close on the reins, pressure is applied until the horse comes once more to a standstill, and again the rider mentally counts to five. Then the horse is again moved forward, and so on, gradually increasing the time and the distance between halts as the horse reacts by flexing his poll and showing that he is responding to training by coming back with less pressure applied on his mouth each time. At the end of ten minutes or so, the horse should be responding easily to the use of the reins, and requiring very little pressure against his mouth.

When trotting and stopping a horse, the things to remember in order to make the exercise effective for both horse and rider: Be sure the horse is stopped in a straight line. Don't let him swing his hindquarters either way.

You cannot continue at this or any other schooling exercise for too long at a time. Remember that the horse's intelligence is a limited one. Schooling exercises—even the simplest ones—impose a severe strain on the horse as he tries to understand what is wanted of him and to yield to the command. Therefore, ten minutes of any schooling exercise is enough. Then let the horse relax on a loose rein.

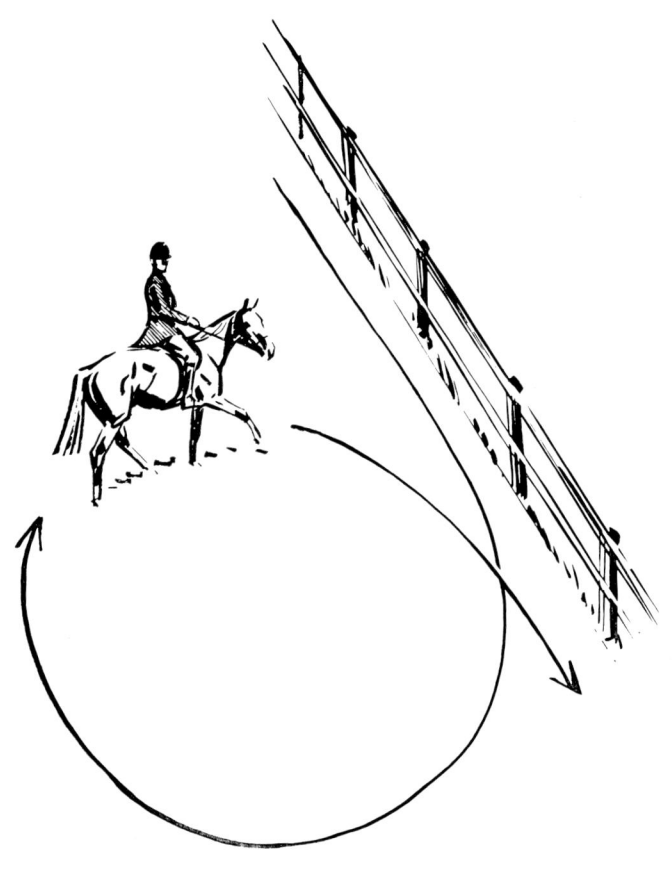

The Circle

The rider being on the track, at the walk, slow trot, trot, or canter, describes a complete circle parallel to the track and retakes the track at the point where he left it—(See illustration).

The diameter of the circle at the walk	1 yard
At the slow or sitting trot	2 yards
At the posting trot	3 yards
At the canter	4 yards

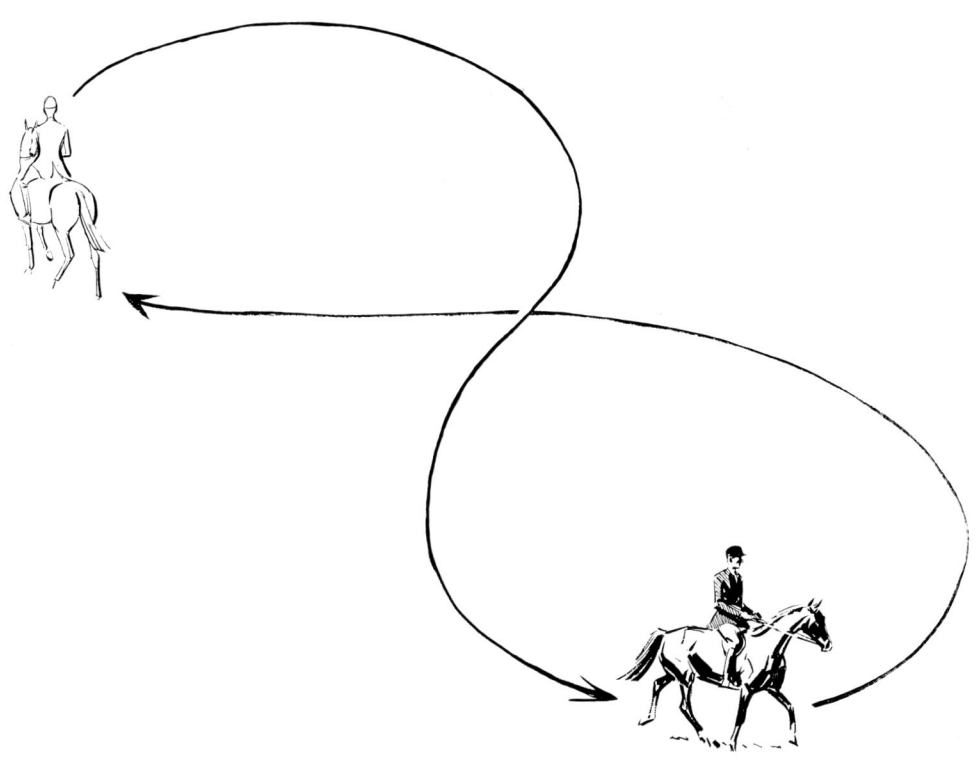

The Figure Eight

This exercise consists of describing the figure of eight first at the walk, the slow trot, the posting trot, and, finally, the canter, with a change of leads in the middle of the figure. At the trot, the rider changes his diagonals. At the canter, he comes down to a slow trot for a step or two before taking the canter on the opposite lead. This assures that the horse is collected, with his hindquarters properly engaged under him, allowing him to take the lead from the hindquarters rather than roll into it from the forehand. Later on, of course, when the rider's controls are working smoothly, the figure eight may be done with a flying change of the lead.

When making the figure eight, note that *both* circles are equal in diameter.

Serpentine

Consists of parallel lines, executed as illustrated. Again the diameter is the same as that of the circle.

When making the serpentine at the trot, the rider changes his diagonals. At the canter, he has the choice of keeping his horse on a false lead or breaking back to a trot and then putting the horse on the correct lead. The flying change of the lead is something I do not recommend to the rider whose aids are not working very smoothly.

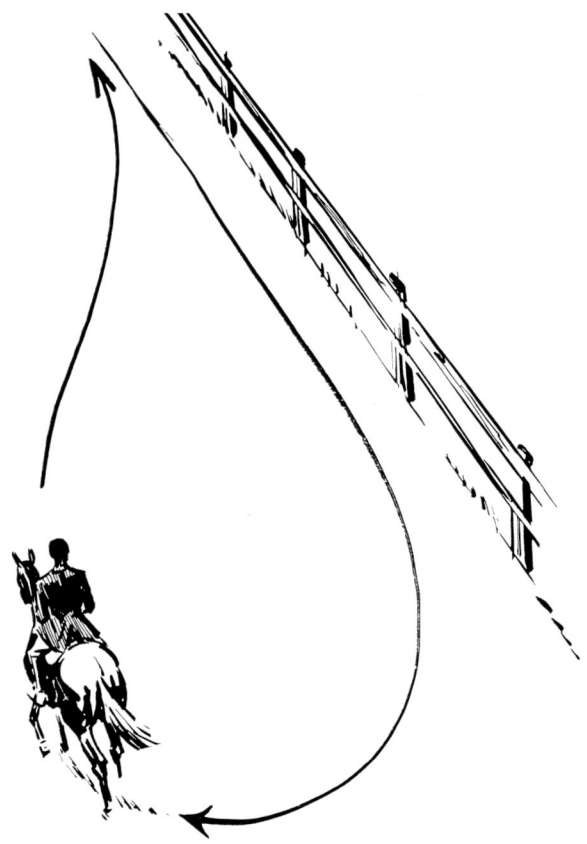

The Half Turn

This movement is an excellent exercise for learning and perfecting the turn on the haunches.

Consists of an about followed by an oblique. Being on the track on the right hand, at the walk, slow trot or trot, the rider describes a right about and then regains the track by the right oblique. At the moment the horse starts the right about, the rider, by applying the right indirect rein in front of the withers and an active left leg, turns the horse on his haunches.

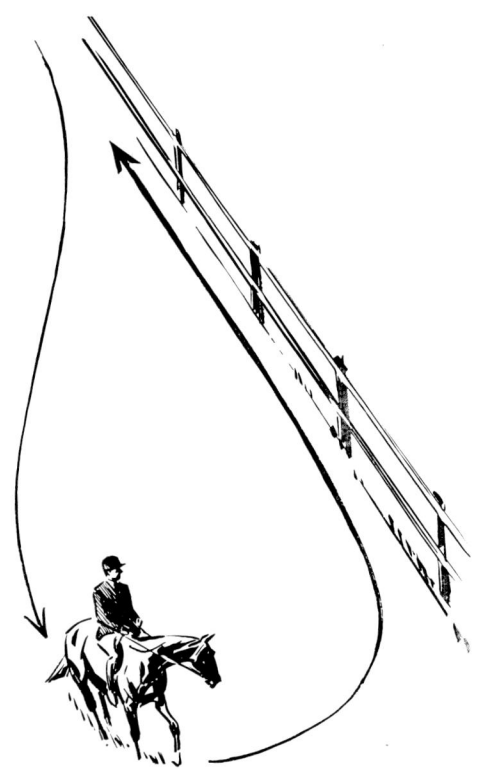

The Half Turn in Reverse

Consists of an oblique followed by an about.

Being on the track on the right hand, at the walk or slow trot, the rider does a right oblique and then, at the proper distance, turns left to regain the track.

At the moment the horse starts the turn, the rider, by increasing the action of the right leg and left indirect rein, has forced the horse to turn on the haunches.

Broken Line

This movement will help soften your horse laterally and at the same time force the rider to use his hands and legs.

Application: Track to the left, use left indirect rein and left leg to come out, right indirect rein and right leg to go back to the track. Continue exercise until horse feels wieldy under you. With this exercise, the rider is doing left and right shoulder-in.

Jumping—Second Grade

The biggest difference between first and second grade jumping is that now the rider, approaching the jump, will use his release at different distances from the jump. First the rider should release six strides before the jump and then five, and so on until he has mastered the art of releasing just for the take-off. The first exercise is to take a course of obstacles keeping the same pace and releasing the horse at the jump. Pace varies with height and width of obstacles.

Another exercise would be to have your horse on a loose rein and ask him to jump with the leg or the voice at the right time of take-off.

Riding a Course of Jumps

By the time the rider is ready to ride a course of jumps, he should be sufficiently advanced and his reactions sufficiently automatic, so there is nothing on his mind but two things: setting and maintaining the pace, and keeping his eyes focused in the direction of movement.

Remember: The horse and rider should be on the alert from the minute they enter the ring until they leave it.

The most important moment in the whole jump occurs three strides before the fence. That is when the horse gives the rider the feeling of any disobedience, such as a refusal or run-out, and when the rider can still prevent it.

When riding a course of jumps without wings, be careful of speed. The faster the horse goes, the faster he is likely to run out and the more difficult he is for the rider to control.

Never add speed to correct a run-out. A run-out is punished and corrected by a sudden, sharp pressure on the rein in the opposite direction from that in which the horse has run out. For a refusal: use your spurs and stick immediately.

Always avoid over-schooling. More horses have been soured through over-schooling than by any other single thing connected with the showing of horses. When your horse has put in a good smooth performance, put him away and let it go at that. When making turns look at the obstacle you are going to take next and not at your horse.

Showing the Hunter

Before starting the first jump, look over the complete course and make a plan in your mind how you are going to ride, in order to show your horse to his best advantage. First, consider the pace you are going to take and hold. Next, consider the distance between obstacles and if it is right for the stride of your horse. If it is not, at some point on your course, you must plan to adjust that stride by either lengthening or shortening it so that your horse approaches the jump just right for a good take off. If you are right and your horse either shortens his stride or tries to increase it just before the take off, be alert and ready for a correction.

If the distance is quite long between obstacles, try and measure your jump at least six strides before the fence so you can lengthen the stride (by releasing your horse and using your legs) or you can shorten the stride (by sitting down in your saddle and adding pressure on your horse's mouth).

For Less Advanced Riders

A very different technique is used. Instead of using the legs for a take off, the rider should use his voice, a light cluck. If your horse does not respond to the cluck, use a bat on him and cluck at the same time while standing still. The association of ideas (the cluck and the bat) will give your horse enough impulsion, so that when used at the right time it will give him impetus for the take off.

If your horse is extremely bold, a release for the take off, while holding an even pace, is the only thing necessary.

A good pace, for most of the horses showing, is about sixteen miles per hour over a four foot outside course. In a riding hall or ring, the pace should be slower, approximately fourteen miles per hour and for a green course (jumps about three foot six) about twelve miles per hour.

Out of doors, in a class calling for brilliancy, the pace, if the horse is capable, should be increased to eighteen miles per hour. However, the majority of horses can not and will not look well and jump safely at this speed, so do not try the impossible.

Budd

PART II

Longeing

By BERTALAN DE NEMETHY, Coach, U.S.E.T.

THERE is a great deal more to longeing a horse properly than most people think. Correct longeing demands a high degree of skill, experience and concentration. In the hands of an experienced trainer, the longe line can accomplish miracles. However, much damage can be done through ignorance or laziness.

Longeing has three principal uses. First, it is helpful in training the young horse to move on the circle with lively, even and relaxed strides at the walk, trot and canter. Secondly, it can be used to help correct certain faults in a horse, such as a stiff back or a loss of elasticity in movement; in other words, it is helpful in *remaking* a horse. Finally, of course, longeing may be used to administer light exercise.

The necessary equipment includes the longe line, which should be 25

to 30 feet long; the longe whip, which should be long enough to enable the trainer standing at the center of the circle to touch the horse with the end of his lash; the surcingle (or a regular saddle) and the side reins (or, for retraining, draw reins).

In correct longeing the trainer will normally remain in the same place in the center of the circle, and only turn on his heels to remain facing the horse. The longe line should extend to the horse's mouth with a light contact, at approximately the same level as the horse's mouth. The remainder of the line should be loosely coiled, and the extreme end slipped over the hand. The longe line is always held on the same side as the direction of movement, i.e., the leading side. The other, following hand will hold the

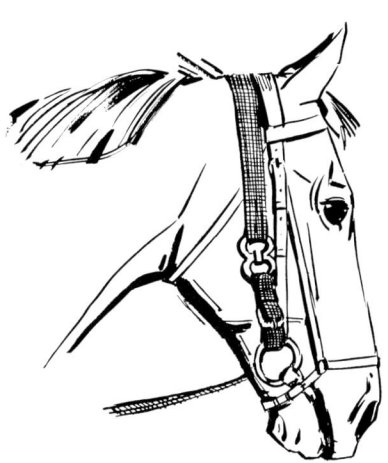

whip, which should be held at about the level of the hocks, and carried just behind the horse's hind legs.

Side lines or draw reins should be adjusted while the horse is standing, and carrying its head and neck naturally; under these circumstances, there should be a light contact.

The trainer will know his longeing is correct when the horse moves exactly on the circle with an even, lively rhythm, its action springy and relaxed, its breathing regular. The animal should neither attempt to take the trainer's hand and pull away from the circle, nor try to move inside the circle and toward the trainer.

The horse is controlled in its actions on the longe line by means of three aids: the longe line itself, through which the hand acts just as the hand of the rider does; the whip, which serves to fulfill the functions of the rider's legs; and the voice. A fine coordination of these three aids will enable the trainer to exercise his influence and control almost as well from the ground as he can from the horse's back. In addition, it is possible to exercise a subtle influence by slightly moving or inclining the body towards the front or rear of the horse.

Actions of longe line include the enlarging and diminishing of the circle by altering the length of the lead, and the parade and half-parade (halt and half-halt).

The principal *actions of the whip* are the driving influence, in which the whip is flicked towards the horse's hocks, from behind, and the pushing-out influence, which is achieved by flicking the whip in an upward motion, from the horse's knees to its shoulder.

The voice can be used to reinforce both the driving and retarding aids, and encourage either greater liveliness, or a slower cadence.

Basic Exercises on the Longe Line
1. The establishment of the basic rhythm of the horse's trot (which will vary according to the individual's construction and temperament).
2. Teaching the horse to extend this basic trot, changing the length of the strides without changing their tempo.
3. Teaching the horse to collect its basic trot.
4. Developing the ordinary canter.
5. Extending the canter.
6. Collecting the canter.
7. Development of the walk.
8. The Parade and half-parade.
9. Transitions between gaits.

Once the horse has learned to find its natural balance on the longe line, the trainer may commence exercising over a single cavaletti. All of his skill must be concentrated on helping the horse to move over the cavaletti without changing its rhythm, and especially without shortening its stride. Should the horse meet the cavaletti out of stride, the correction must always be made by stretching the neck, and extending the shoulder. In other words, the correction must always be made *forward*.

All longeing exercises should be done on both hands equally. Since work on a circle can easily become monotonous, the trainer must take pains to vary his demands as much as possible to prevent staleness on the part of the horse. It is wise to alternate the direction in which the horse starts his work every day; and it is also important to permit sufficient opportunities for the horse to rest and relax for a few strides.

Longeing the Rider

A century ago the riding master Steinbreck stated, "The secret, or key to the art of riding is really very simple: make your horse straight, and ride him forward."

The words are indeed simple, but training of horse to be "straight" and to accept the driving aids is not nearly as simple as the words. Moreover, the techniques of dressage which can enable us to accomplish this must be studied and practised as thoroughly as the techniques of any other specialized skill. (Indeed, it seems strange that many people, who would never think of trying to drive a car without first learning how, expect to ride a horse without learning what to do or how to do it.)

If one is to succeed in making his horse's entire structure straight, so that its weight will be equally distributed on all four legs, and so that it can achieve its natural balance, while carrying the rider on its back, he must first learn to sit correctly on the horse. By the same token, if one is to "ride the horse forward" he must develop an immediate and obedient response to his driving aids—and to apply these aids correctly one must know how to sit on the horse in such a way that the influences of the seat and legs are unmistakably clear and entirely under the rider's control.

For how can the rider avoid disturbing the balance of the horse and at the same time influence it to move forward if he does not have a seat that is both relaxed and firm, enabling him to control his aids and to never unintentionally disturb the horse's balance? And how can the rider "ride forward" by pushing the horse with his legs and leading it with his hands if neither his hands nor his legs are truly independent of his seat?

The faulty seat precludes any real accomplishment in the development of the horse's training because it forces the rider to use his hands and legs to hang on with, instead of acting as aids. Thus it is obvious that all the arts of riding are based on the foundation of a sound seat, this, experience has taught us, is most readily achieved by placing the rider on a longe-line, without stirrups.

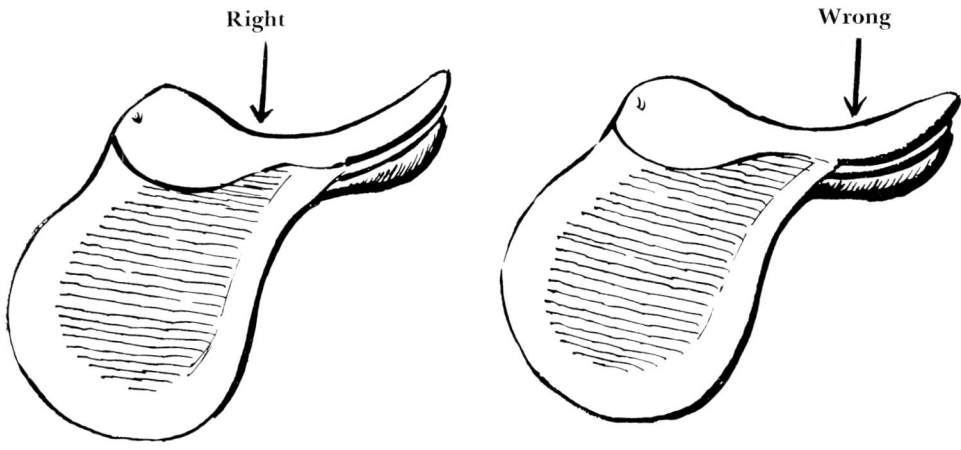

The requirements for correcting the rider's seat by longeing are:

1. A horse which moves reasonably well, and has learned to move evenly and quietly with side-lines on both hands.
2. A coach who clearly understands the form and mechanics of a correct seat and is able to correct every deviation of the rider.
3. A correctly constructed saddle, so designed and so padded that the deepest part of the saddle is sufficiently far forward. (See illustration)

For the greatest benefits to be derived from this type of exercise, it is important that the rider has nothing at all to do with the control of the horse; the horse, in sidelines with the regular snaffle rein knotted and lying on its neck, should be subject to regulation only by the person longeing it. The stirrups have, of course, been removed from the saddle.

The "coach" must constantly verify:

1. That the rider sits squarely and evenly on his "seat bones"—and not on the base of his spine, or on his crotch.
2. That the position of the upper body is vertical, and gently coordinates with the horse's movements; the rider's shoulders, hip joint and heels should be in the same vertical line.
3. That the back is slightly stressed (or "braced").
4. That thigh, knee and calf are held flat against the saddle, and not permitted to turn outward so that the contact would come on the back part of them, rather than the inside.
5. That the heels are depressed and kept close to the horse's ribs, yet without excessive forcing or tension. (The rider should feel that he "carries his toes".)

6. That the slightly vaulted chest, relaxed and supple shoulders, and natural, erect carriage of the head contribute to an overall impression of easy elegance of bearing.
7. That the arms are held relaxed, close to the body, with the forearm describing a straight line from the elbow to the horse's mouth, and that the hands are close together, the fingers closed on imaginary reins, the palms turned slightly inward.

(The above elements of the rider's position are listed in descending order of "urgency" from the coach's point of view—for without No. 1, nothing else can be correct, and so forth.)

Indispensable as longeing is to the development of a correct seat, it is unfortunately not an automatic process—and a half-hour of longeing daily, done incorrectly, can as easily ruin a seat as make one. Thus there is no point in prolonging a rider's suffering past the point that he or his coach have lost ability or willingness to concentrate patiently and persistently.

Whenever the rider's seat is wrong—and this will be most of the time at the beginning—he should assist himself by holding onto the saddle, the outside hand on the pommel, the inside hand on the cantle, until a correct seat position has been restored. He should dispense with this assistance *only as long as his position remains correct,* though this period will hardly exceed a few seconds at the beginning. Later on, of course, the rider will be able to maintain a correct position, unaided, for longer and longer periods of time —but it cannot be too strongly stressed, that nothing is accomplished by trying to reestablish a correct position without taking hold of the saddle, and thus the teacher must insist on this "seat correction" every time the rider begins to lose his balance and thus his seat.

There are many possible variations of particular suppling exercises which can be employed while the rider is on the longe line in accordance with his particular requirements. Their intelligent employment is a challenge to the imagination and experience of the coach, who will not follow any slavish pattern of arm or body rotation but will isolate those particular muscles and joints which the rider fails to relax sufficiently, and invent appropriate suppling exercises.

Seat correction work on the longe line should be accomplished at all three gaits, with emphasis on the trot. Though the first few instruction periods will probably be rather short, the length of the longeing work should be increased up to a maximum of about 45 minutes.

Carl Klein

PART III

Fox Hunting

By Mrs. John J. McDonald, Ex-MFH, Meadowbrook Hunt

THAT fox-hunting is not a competitive sport is a fact which should be known to all. Unfortunately, however, in the excitement of a fast hunt, it is frequently recognized by too few. The purpose of fox-hunting is to seek out, chase and kill or put to ground a fox with a pack of hounds; not to see how many fences you can take in a day, or how fast you can get to them. If that is your desire, I would recommend that you stay away from fox-hunting and take a good, long cross-country ride instead. But if you are going fox-hunting, then you are going out to combine two of the most thrilling sports in the world; galloping a good horse cross-country, and watching hounds work.

The Hunter: Assuming that you are no great rider, but are able to handle any reasonably mannered horse with satisfaction to yourself and no harm to him, we will deal first with your horse, for he will be the most important part of the hunt to you.

You may be the lucky owner of a hunter; you may be contemplating buying one; or you may have to hire or borrow a mount; but no matter what your status, there is only one horse to hunt, and that is the reasonably mannered one. No one knows how many people have been literally driven out of the hunting field by riding horses they could not control. "Handsome is as handsome does" was never truer than here, and for the beginner especially, a well-mannered, aged hunter which knows the business backwards, and takes good care of himself, is a "must". He may be no dream to look at, but if he brings you safely home after a long, hard day, how much better he will appear to you than the head-strong, rattle-headed beauty who not only wore you to a frazzle, but quite likely gave you a nasty fall in the bargain! Of course there are all kinds of horses for all types of hunting. The big-striding thoroughbred that is at home in an open galloping country is far from a pleasant mount in a trappy, close-quartered one, with narrow panels and large Fields. For happy hunting under such conditions the cold-blooded horse with the big, careful jump and the disposition to wait his turn at fences is a far more satisfactory mount.

The Hounds: Too few people understand the importance of hounds and overestimate the importance of jumping during a hunt. As a result, a Master is often irritated to the point of asking a noisy, talkative rider to turn his horse around and go home. The success of a hunt is almost entirely due to the skill of the huntsman and the ability of the hounds. You will have a good day's hunting, or a bad one, depending largely upon the co-operation between the two. Much of hunting tradition centers around the hounds, and even the rank beginner must know enough about it not to ruin a day's sport for the rest of the Field.

The Master: As a rule, the Master is someone who has lived in that country and hunted with that pack for many years. He is often the one who contributes large sums of money to keep the country paneled and guarantees land owners that they will be properly reimbursed for any damage to fields, fences, or crops. He is a man with a background of hunting tradition, and a person who loves all of it sufficiently to work hard at the job of building up and keeping a good hunt. The Master is respected and deferred to at all times. Like the skipper on a ship, for as long as you are in the hunting field, his word is law. Sometimes the Master hunts the hounds himself, in which case there will also be a Field Master, who is in charge of the Field, thereby freeing the Master from those duties so that he may devote his entire attention to hunting the hounds.

The Hunt-Secretary: Usually the Hunt-Secretary is an amateur who contributes a lot of time to keeping the Hunt books, handling the finances, paying the bills, collecting the subscriptions and capping fees, answering all manner of mail, and sending out the fixture cards. He must also keep an accurate day-by-day record of the people hunting.

The Huntsman: The hounds are handled and hunted by the Huntsman, and he is responsible for them. It takes a good Huntsman years to learn how to work a pack of fox-hounds. The Hunt Club has begun by spending many thousands of dollars building up a good pack. It is up to the Huntsman to teach them obedience, and he in turn must understand every sound they make. It is not important to the rider who has just begun to hunt to know any of this, but it is not only important, but also essential for him to realize what the Huntsman is trying to do. The hounds speak in many different tones and voices which is referred to as "making music". It sounds like a babble of noise to the uninitiated, but even the slightest change of a hound's tone has told the Huntsman something about the fox he is seeking, and even a small noise from the Field can throw him off. For this reason, it is important that you hunt on a quiet, obedient horse. A restless horse, moving and stamping the ground, can drown out the sound of a far-off hound.

The Whipper-In: The Whip, as the Whipper-In is commonly called, may be either amateur or professional. There is usually a First and a Second Whip in a Hunt. Their duties are many and varied, but have only one purpose, and that is to help the Huntsman in every way. They keep the pack together when hacking along roads; bring up the stragglers in the course of a hunt; turn hounds back to the Huntsman when they run "riot", (that is pursue some game other than a fox); and keep watch on the edge of a covert which is being drawn in order to notify the Huntsman in case a fox tries to steal away.

The Field: Members, and subscribers to the Hunt, and their guests, comprise the Field. Their position in the hunting field is usually based on seniority rights. The older members—older in point of membership, not age—stay up in front. All considerate riders who find themselves out on horses they are not sure they can control, or on green horses which might be expected to refuse or to run out, stay behind. It is well to bear in mind that the hunting field is not the place in which to school a green horse. If you have a horse that kicks, you should have a red ribbon in his tail and remain in the rear.

Hunting Seasons: Cub-hunting (early season hunting of young foxes by young hounds for education) usually starts in August, after crops are out of the ground. Formal hunting, as a rule, begins sometime in October when the weather is cooler and hounds and horses fit enough for a long day. The hunting season is extended as long as possible, and if the winter is mild, hunting is sometimes continued right through March, until Spring planting.

The Meet: The place where hounds and Field gather to hunt is called the Meet. A notice called a "Fixture Card" is sent to all members and subscribers telling them where and when the Hunt will meet during the season. The place is changed as frequently as possible in order to keep hunting over new country. You should arrive at least half an hour early in order to have time for any last minute attentions to horse or self, and be certain of being in the saddle ready to move off at the appointed time.

If you are a visitor, you will introduce yourself to the Hunt Secretary, and pay your capping fee. Everyone hunting, upon arrival at the Meet, should ride up to the Master and bid him "Good Morning."

The Hunt Subscription: The annual payment required by a Hunt for the privilege of a season's hunting with that pack is called the Hunt Subscription. The amount varies with different Hunts.

Capping Fee: The charge for one day's hunting, made to a visitor who is not a subscriber, is called a Capping Fee. It is a tradition begun in England centuries ago, when hunts were not organized, and the hunt servant went about with his cap collecting whatever anyone cared to contribute to the Hunt.

Hunt Member and Subscriber: A member is always a subscriber, but a subscriber is not necessarily a member. To join a Hunt one must be first invited to subscribe by the Master, but to become a regular member is far more difficult. With full membership comes the right to wear the Hunt buttons and colors. Each season the Master grants permission for colors to be given to subscribers thought worthy of them, but this permission is charily given. To earn one's colors, it is usually necessary to have hunted faithfully two to five years with the Hunt in question and to have proved oneself to be a sportsman in the true sense of the word.

Hunting Attire

Informal: During the cub-hunting season, informal attire, often called "Rat-Catcher," is worn. For either lady or gentleman, it usually consists of tweed coat, any neutral shade of breeches with brown boots or jodhpurs. A hard hat is always recommended for safety.

Formal: During the regular hunting season, the attire worn by both members and subscribers should be formal.

Gentlemen Subscriber: A regular riding coat with plain buttons, in black or dark gray should be worn with boots of plain black calf and a black bowler with hat guard. The coat may also be a frock coat, a cutaway (swallow tail), or a shad belly, in which case the boots should have patent leather tops and the hat be a hunting silk one. Breeches should be buff, stone, canary or brown. Waistcoat should be canary with plain brass buttons. Stock must be white with plain gold safety pin; gloves yellow or white string, chamois or brown pigskin; spurs blunt, with black spur straps; bootgarters to match boots; hunting whip leather covered with brown leather thong and colored lash.

Gentlemen Member: Any of the above coats may be worn, except that the coat and vest buttons should be engraved with the Hunt insignia. The alternative is a scarlet hunt coat similar to that of the Master, with brass coat and vest buttons engraved with the Hunt insignia. A hunting silk hat must be worn. Breeches should be white; boots black with mahogany tops; and boot garters white. All other appointments should be the same as for a gentleman subscriber.

Lady Subscriber: (Astride) Attire should be the same as for a gentleman subscriber, except that the coat may also be navy in color.

Lady Member: (Astride) Attire should be same as for a lady subscriber, except that the coat and vest buttons should be engraved with the Hunt insignia, and the Hunt colors worn on the collar.

Lady Subscriber: (Side Saddle) Habit should be of any dark color with breeches matching, or of a neutral shade. Vest is usually white or canary and boots should be black without tops. Either a bowler or hunting silk hat, depending on the type of coat, may be worn, with hat guard, unless veil is used.

Lady Member: (Side Saddle) Habit should be the same as above, except that the coat and vest buttons should be engraved with Hunt insignia and Hunt colors worn on the collar.

Hunt Caps: Those eligible to wear hunt caps are: Juniors under eighteen, the Master, the Hunt Secretary, the Hunt Staff, and ex-Masters. Everyone else should wear a black bowler, or with a scarlet, cutaway, or frock coat, a hunting silk hat.

Hunting Cries and Sounds: When it is time for the Hunt to start, the Master directs the Huntsman to blow his horn, and this is the signal for the Field to move off. Later, when hounds have found a fox, and the Huntsman sees where they are headed, he sounds several short notes on his horn, and this means "gone away." The Master follows at a suitable distance with the Field behind him. Sometimes the Field is crowded into a narrow road, or a clump of woods, and the Huntsman is watching hounds and waiting for their next move. They may turn and come back along the same path, at which time you will hear the cry of "Master, please," "Huntsman, please," and when you do, back your horse off the road keeping his head, not his hindquarters, toward

the path along which the Master, hounds, or Huntsman will be coming. Other sounds you will hear are "Ware hole" or "Ware wire," and when the signal comes to you, pass it along to the rider behind you promptly, as this may prevent an accident. If the Field has checked, and someone happens to see the fox breaking cover, he cries out, "Tallyho" and indicates to the Master where he saw the fox and in which direction it was going. These are the more familiar hunting cries, and the only ones the novice needs to know for his own and others protection.

Hunting Language: Hounds are never called dogs, except when referring to the dog-pack as distinct from the bitch-pack. In counting, never refer to two or three hounds, but always to a couple, or a couple and a half. Hounds never bark, but speak to a line—this is called owning the line. A hound never has a tail, it is always a stern. When hounds are becoming actively interested in a line, and their sterns move quickly from side to side, they are said to be feathering. After this they may sweep away on a line and give tongue, which is called the cry of the hounds, or music. Any dog encountered in the course of a hunt, which is not a fox-hound, is called a cur-dog.

In counting foxes, never refer to two or three foxes, but always to a brace, or to a brace and a half.

General Courtesy Hints: You will always be welcome in a hunt, if you remember that there are certain customs to be respected.

Therefore:

Do not talk at a check while hounds are working. There will be other intervals while hacking between coverts when it is permissible to talk, but when hounds are working out a line, the rule is—"Silence, please." If you are a new subscriber, stay to the rear.

If your horse refuses a fence, pull over to one side, and get in again at the end of the line.

Do not crowd when coming down to fences. Allow two horses lengths between you and the horse ahead, so that if the horse or rider goes down, there will be no danger of your horse stepping on him. Wait your turn at fences. Do not cut in on the horse ahead of you, as serious accidents can result.

Never take a jump until hounds have cleared it and are well out of the way.

If a hunt servant is lowering a jump, wait until he has finished. Do not try to keep up with the Field. Wait and catch up later.

If someone has a fall, stop long enough to be sure that he is all right, and then, if necessary, see that a car is sent back for him.

Keep your distance, but keep up. By letting your horse drop back in a narrow path, you run the risk of not only losing the Field, yourself, but of causing everyone behind you to do the same thing.

Do not take any more jumps than you have to, and never jump a large fence when you can take a small one. The rest of the Field is out to watch hounds work so, if you want to "lark," do not go hunting.

If you cannot hold your horse, *Go Home!* There is nothing more dangerous in the hunting field than a horse out of control. He risks not only his rider's neck, but also endangers everyone else in the Field.

At the end of the day ride up to the Master and thank him for a pleasant day's hunting.

A visitor should write a "Thank you" note to the Master a day or two after the Hunt.

If you will abide by these few rules of courtesy, which have been dictated by the tradition inherent in fox-hunting, you will not only discover one of the greatest pleasures open to a horseman, but also you will be a welcome addition to any hunt.

Marjorie B. McDonald

SECTION FOUR

The Horse

Part I

HEAD	89
LEG	90
COLOR GUIDE	90

Part II

SELECTING A HORSE	91
CONFORMATION	94

Part III

UNSOUNDNESS	95

Part IV

VETERINARY PREPARATION OF THE HORSE AND MAINTENANCE OF CONDITION DURING COMPETITION by Dr. Joseph C. O'Dea	102
PAIN KILLERS AND TRANQUILIZERS by Dr. Joseph C. O'Dea	105

THE HORSE

PART I

Head

- **Star:** White mark between the eyes.
- **Snip:** White mark between the nostrils.
- **Stripe:** White mark extending down face to bridge of nose.
- **Blaze:** An exaggerated white stripe not including the eyes or nostrils.
- **Bald:** White face including the eyes and nostrils or a portion thereof.

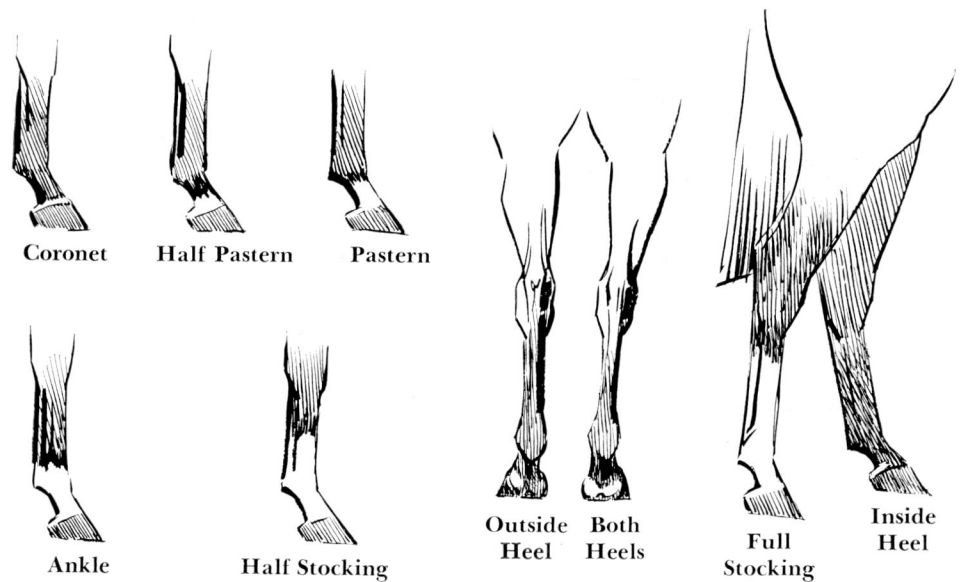

Leg

Terms: Use "near" in place of "left," and "off" in place of "right."
Ankle: The joint between the pastern and cannon bone.
Fetlock: The lower rear portion of ankle.

Color Guide

Bay: This varies from a light yellowish tan (light bay), to a dark rich shade almost brown (dark bay). Should be described simply as "Bay," "Light Bay" or "Dark Bay." Black mane, tail, and legs.

Brown: This is sometimes difficult to tell from black or dark bay, but can be distinguished by noting the fine tan or brown hairs on the muzzle or flanks.

Black: If any doubt arises in determining between dark brown and black, the black can be determined by noting the fine black hairs on the muzzle.

Chestnut: This varies from a light washy yellow (light chestnut) to a dark liver color (dark chestnut), between which come the brilliant red gold and copper shades. Never have black mane, tail or points. Should be described simply as "Chestnut," "Light Chestnut" or "Dark Chestnut."

Dun: This varies from mouse color to beige, and very generally is accompanied by black points and black stripe down back.

Gray: This is a mixture or white hairs and black, sometimes scarcely distinguishable from black at birth, getting lighter with age.

Roan: This is a mixture of white hairs and chestnut; or white and bay.

PART II

Selecting A Horse

BEING able to know and judge a horse's conformation with any degree of skill or accuracy is beyond the knowledge and ability of the average rider. When you set out to buy a horse, you should put yourself in the hands of a dealer or professional horseman in whom you have confidence, and be guided by his advice. A majority of bad horse deals are not the result of dishonest horse trading, but the result of the rider's over-estimation of his own riding ability so he finds himself over-mounted; or the result of trying to purchase a single horse to fill too many different needs and riding requirements.

Whether you are going to hire a horse, or to buy one of your own, the first thing to do is to make a reasonable estimate of your own riding ability. Good horses make good riders; a good horse enables even a mediocre rider to look good; but bad riders ruin good horses. The surest way to lose courage and security on a horse and start the development of bad hands is to find yourself over-mounted. When selecting a horse which you hope to enjoy for an hour's pleasant hacking or for years of enjoyable hunting and jumping, never over-estimate your own riding ability. Horses habits can be changed, but their dispositions remain the same. A bold horse is always a bold horse, not even cutting down on his feed will make him a really quiet mount.

If you have to err, try to err on the side of getting something that is a little less horse than you think you can safely manage. The beginner is far safer with a horse he has to urge than with one he has to hold. Until a secure seat and reasonably steady hands have been developed, it is well to be mounted on a horse that does not require too much control. The second consideration in choosing the horse you are to ride, or to own, is deciding what you really want in a horse—a quiet hack, a horse that can hunt well and also show a little, or a horse that can be shown and jumped, but that probably will not be too well-behaved in the company of the hunt field.

Every once in a while, of course, we do happen upon a combination of the horse that hunts and shows, hacks and jumps, with equal ability in each field. Since such a horse is the exception rather than the rule, make up your own mind what it is you want from your horse. The horse that hunts quietly and jumps well in company does not, as a rule, jump well alone. Many riding accidents would never have happened if people could control the false pride that makes them almost ashamed to ask for a quiet horse. I have never been able to figure out why poor riders think they can control a high-spirited horse, when, by their own admission, they can't even make a quiet horse move forward!

The good horseman is *always* mounted on a quiet horse, because whatever horse he is on seems quiet. Until you have reached the stage where your controls are able to function independently and automatically under any and all conditions, always ask for a quiet horse. If you're really good enough to ride the other kind, you're good enough to get a good ride out of any horse.

When you get ready to buy a horse, have confidence in the man from whom you are buying! Go to someone who has seen you ride and knows your riding ability. Tell him frankly your price limit and what you expect in the way of performance. If necessary, sacrifice age to temperament, and looks to jumping skill. Of the four or five things that you want a horse to do well for you, if you get a horse that does *one* of those things really well, consider yourself lucky.

Meanwhile, I think you will feel better about either hiring or buying a horse for your own riding enjoyment, if you know a little bit about a horse's conformation and how his good and bad points will affect your comfort and safety while in the saddle. Perfection is what we seek but seldom find. So remember that a good horse is one with many good points, some indifferent points, and no really bad points. Any number of good points in a horse cannot compensate for one really bad point. The body cannot be stronger than its weakest part. Some confirmation faults, while certainly not desirable, are not too important. Others are important enough to render the horse either unfit or unsafe.

Another thing to remember in checking your horse's good and bad points is that "handsome is as handsome does." It is true that a horse cannot be too deep through the chest, but getting a good, deep-chested horse, with plenty of room for heart and lungs to work perfectly, is no good for the rider if the heart itself isn't there. There are "chicken-hearted" horses just as there are "chicken-hearted" people. Sometimes, this is just a result of poor training, and the horse having been put at obstacles that are too much for him. When this is the case, it is comparatively easy to restore the horse's confidence and "nerve." But there *are* some horses who simply do not have heart, who have to be whipped and spurred over every fence and who take advantage of every opportunity to quit or to run out. In a jumping horse, that kind of disposition is something that would completely nullify a dozen good conformation points. A good horse for you is a horse that is physically and temperamentally suited to your riding needs. He is a horse who can perform well, stand up under the amount of work he is going to be asked to do, and so constructed that the rider has a pleasant, enjoyable time for the hours he is in the saddle.

Some of our top conformation hunters will not measure up to those requirements, but top conformation hunters are only expected to strip well when shown in hand and to perform creditably under the artificial conditions of the show ring. They are neither asked, nor expected, to do a day's work in the hunt field, carry the timid or uncertain rider over fences, or to perform smoothly and quietly enough for the young horsemanship rider to look well in horsemanship events.

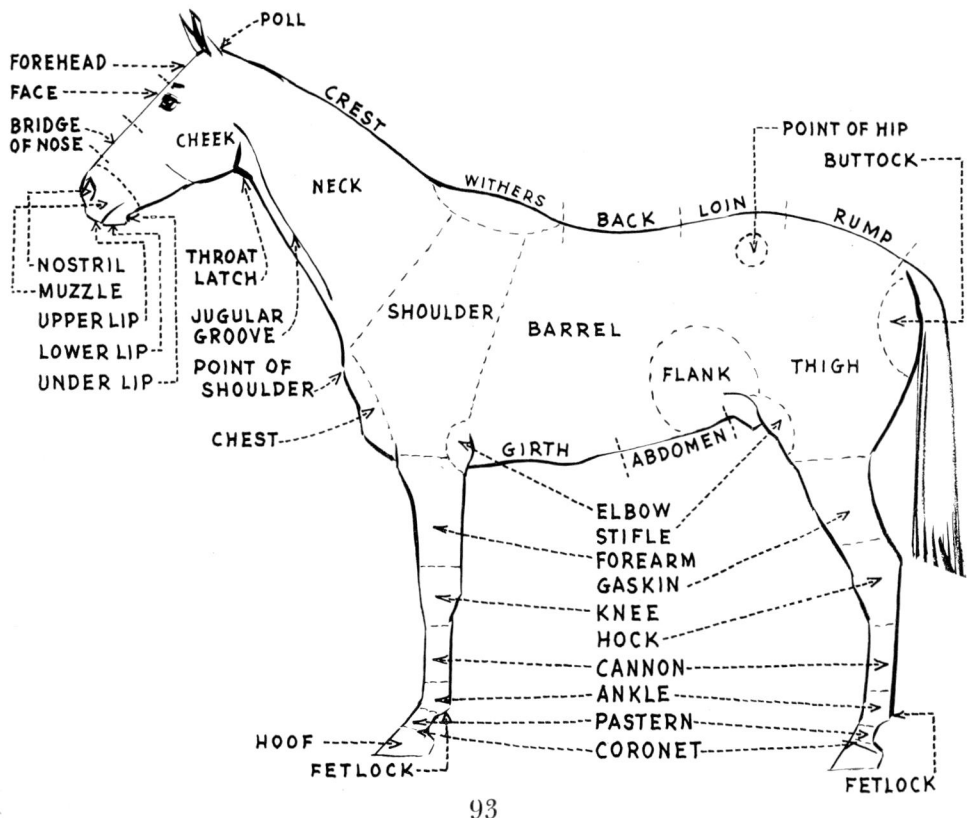

Conformation

	Faults	*Good points*
Head	Lop-ears Pig-eyed Roman nosed Dish-faced	Small ears, set well apart Broad forehead Eyes large, set far apart Face, lean and fine
Neck	Eye-neck Bull-necked	Long, and of a thickness consistent with the rest of the horse's body
Withers	Mutton-withered	Moderately high, not too thin nor bulky with muscle
Shoulder	Straight	Long and sloping
Cannon	Too long Tied in below knee Calf-kneed Knock-kneed Bowlegged	Short and strong Broad and flat
Pastern	Coon-footed (long pastern) Short and stubby	Moderate length Correct slope
Foot	Contracted Toed-out, or splay footed Toed-in	In proportion to size of horse; heels should be broad, of moderate height
Back	Sway back Roach back	Straight, not too long
Chest	Barrel-chested Slab-sided	Of moderate breadth, and cannot be too deep
Loin	Long coupled	No more than three fingers' width between last rib and point of hip
Barrel	Herring-gutted or shad-bellied	Well let down
Rump	Goose-rumped or Rainy-day croup Hips too prominent	Good length, moderate width and slope
Hock	Cow-hocked Tied in below hock	Clean, well defined Bones large and prominent, no roughness or puffiness
Cannon (Hind)	Sickle-hocked Curby hock	Slightly longer than front cannon; one inch greater bone measurement

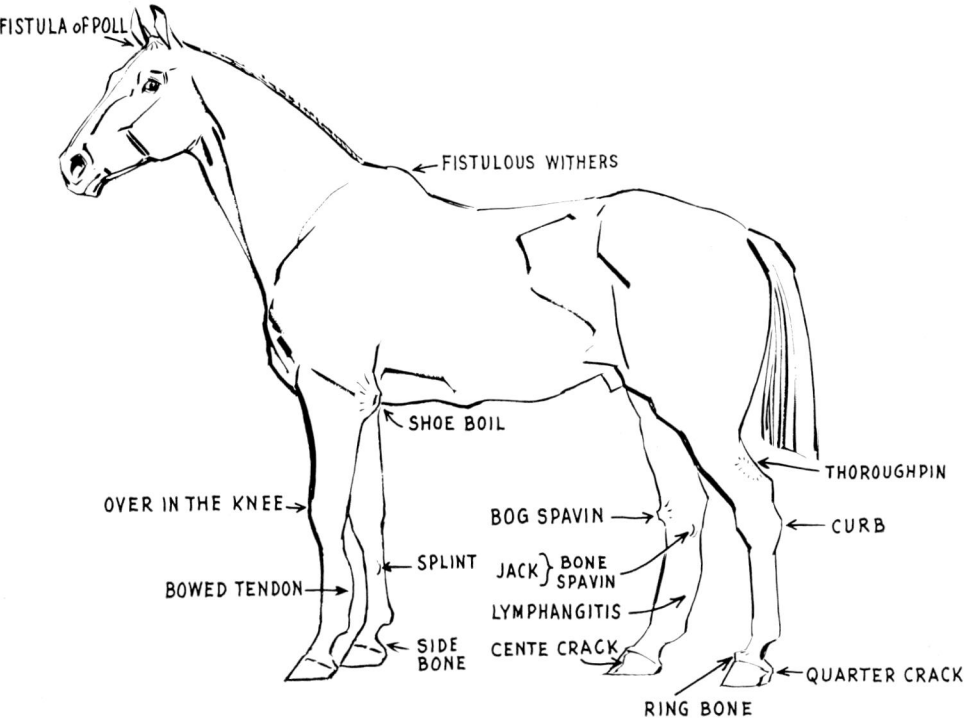

PART III

Unsoundness

FEW animals are free from unsoundness, but a horse is serviceably-sound when the unsoundness is not of a type, or a degree, to impair the horse's ability to perform. Small splints, wind puffs, or a small white spot on the cornea are all unsoundnesses that do not impair the horse's serviceability.

Following is a list of the more common unsoundnesses, their definition and their description. By comparing this list with the accompanying chart, you will quickly see the part of the body that is attacked and the physical appearance of the individual unsoundnesses:

Periodic Ophthalmia: Commonly known as "Moon blindness." Can either be acute or chronic, attacks the whole eye, recurring at more or less frequent intervals and usually resulting in total blindness after several attacks. During the attack, the eye is swollen, the cornea appears white or cloudy, tears flow freely, and the eyelids are closed to keep out light. The cause is unknown, but it is wise to consider this disease contagious.

Feather: Is a white scar on the transparent cornea, and is not serious unless the scar is such as to interfere with the horse's vision.

Fistula of the Poll: Or "Poll evil." A swelling in the region of the poll, which eventually abscesses and often discharges pus through one or more openings. Caused by injury.

Wind-Broken: It becomes noticeable when the animal is galloped for any length of time, and is characterized by the slightly roaring sound of wind being drawn into the lungs. It may result from sudden and excessive overwork, diseases such as pneumonia and influenza. A horse so affected is generally rendered unfit for any work that calls for long gallops, such as hunting, hunter trials, and Olympic riding. Surgery to correct or alleviate the condition is successful in about 50% of the cases.

Fistula of the Withers: A swelling in the region of the withers, followed by an abscess which may discharge pus through one or more openings. A difficult condition to treat, and even when the active infection has been healed, the scar tissue which results from this type of infection often leaves the animal stiff in the shoulders.

Sweeny: Atrophy (shrinking) resulting from paralysis of one or more of the muscles covering the shoulder blade. Since it is usually caused by an injury to the large nerve of these muscles, it is a condition found more often in draft horses than in riding horses.

Shoe Boil: Otherwise known as a "capped elbow." An enlargement of the bursa on the point of the elbow, caused by bruising with a long heeled shoe while lying down, or by being allowed to lie down in a stall with insufficient bedding.

Knee Sprung: Or "over in the knee." Sometimes a congenital unsoundness may also be fault of conformation with no unsoundness present, and sometimes caused by a tendon injury or an inflammation of the knee joint. Young horses are frequently knee sprung, but will usually straighten up with proper care. In older horses, this condition is often a result of a horse tied-in below the knee, which predisposes him to inflammation and a shortening of the flexor tendon. Raising Heel excessively is frequently contributory.

Bowed Tendons: An unsoundness resulting from the terrific strain placed on the tendon or from a sudden blow on tendon. Also caused by a horse jumping out of thick mud or other heavy going. It is characterized by an enlargement of the flexor tendons and/or the suspensory ligament in the cannon region, and is considered a serious defect.

Splint: A bony growth along the side of the cannon bone. Often causes lameness while forming, but once the splint has set, the lameness disappears unless the splint is of such a size and location to cause friction on the tendon. Splints seldom develop on animals over ten years old and usually appear before the horse is seven years old.

Bucked Shin: A bony enlargement on the front surface of the cannon bone. Another condition often found among young race horses and the result of unusual concussion in bony column. After the acute inflammation has subsided, the bony enlargement which is left seldom causes lameness.

Ringbone: A bony enlargement in the region of the pastern. It may appear on the long pastern bone, the short pastern bone, or both. In the more severe cases, the enlargement may completely ring the bone. Small and weak pasterns, particularly those that are short, upright and stumpy, are especially prone to ringbone, which is caused by sprains, blows, wounds or concussion and from faulty nutrition. Not all ringbones cause permanent lameness, but in most cases the lameness is both severe and permanent, resisting all forms of treatment once mechanical interference has been established.

Sidebone: A bulging of both the coronary band and the hoof wall over the affected cartilage. A condition which affects the forefeet almost exclusively causing lameness while the condition is coming on, but permitting the horse to go back to work again as soon as the sidebone is set (calcified).

Enlarged Sesamoids: A bony enlargement on the back surface of the fetlock joint. The enlargement is caused by a chronic inflammation of the tissue that surrounds the sesamoid bones, causing the tissue to ossify and resulting in a roughening of the smooth articular surface and the groove for the flexor tendons. This is a serious unsoundness, and one that sometimes causes an incurable lameness in the horse.

Quarter Crack: or a fracture of the hoof wall at the quarter. The pinching of the sensitive laminae in the crevice, and the resulting inflammation cause a painful lameness. Contracted heels, dry feet, concussion, poor blacksmithing and fast work on hard roads may cause this condition.

Navicular Disease: An inflammation of the articular surface of the navicular bone. Concussion from high action, straight shoulders and pasterns and much work on hard ground are the principal contributing causes. The symptoms are lameness, stumbling and stilted gaits, and pointing of the toe when resting, finally reaching a stage where the horse refuses to move forward at all. One of the most difficult of the unsoundnesses to diagnose, and usually only discovered through a process of elimination.

Dropped Sole: A flattening of the sole which produces chronic lameness. The wall of the foot is generally wavy and often concave (or dished) at the toe when viewed from the side, and results from one or more attacks of laminitis.

Corns: Injury and alteration of the sole between bar and the quarter, usually the result of bad shoeing, contracted heels, sidebones, improper trimming of the foot.

Thrush: A disease which attacks the frog of the foot and is characterized by the deterioration of the frog and is accompanied by a singular putrid odor. It is one of the easiest diseases to detect, and one of the most unnecessary, since it is generally the result of carelessness and neglect and may be so severe as to render patient permanently lame.

Knocked-Down Hip: A fracture of the wing of the pelvis, the affected side appearing lower than the normal one. The condition is most easily detected when standing directly behind the animal.

Stringhalt: An unsoundness whose cause no one has been able to prove or to define. It occurs more frequently in old animals, does not render the horse unserviceable, and is manifested by a spasmodic flexion of the hind leg which is most noticeable when the horse is first taken from the stable or asked to back.

Capped Hock: An enlargement of the point of the hock, often caused by bruises resulting from stable kicking or shipping and seldom causing permanent lameness.

Bone Spavin: or "Jack." A bony enlargement on the inside and lower portions of the hock joint. May be caused by faulty conformation, sprain or concussion. The resultant lameness is caused by a roughening of the articular surfaces of the lower hock bones. Some horses have spavins and suffer no lameness from them, while others are rendered permanently lame and useless.

Bog Spavin: A distension of the joint capsule of the hock joint, seen at the inner and upper portions of the front of the hock. Seen most frequently in horses with rather straight hocks, it does not cause lameness except occasionally, in the acute stages. Abnormal nutrition and insufficient exercise frequently cause bog spavin in young animals.

Thoroughpin: A distension of the synovial sheath of the deep flexor tendon which causes a fluctuating swelling on both sides, just in front of the point of the hock and beneath the tendon of Achilles. Small thoroughpins show a bulging on the outside only and are commonly found in coarse or common bred horses that have worked hard. The condition is not apt to cause lameness unless some unusual strain brings on an extension of the sheath.

Curb: A chronic thickening of the flexor tendon sheath and plantar ligament on the back border of the hock. When viewed from the side, the back line of a curby hock appears rounded instead of straight. It seldoms causes lameness.

Summary: Lameness is a symptom, not a cause. Lameness in a horse is something that should be investigated promptly. A horse's lameness is the outer manifestation of some functional or structural disorder. Any of these unsoundnesses which I have listed here may be the cause of your horse's lameness, and knowing what to look for, and where to look for it, may help you discover the cause of his unsoundness. But treating that unsoundness should always be left to the veterinarian, not to grooms or to well-meaning friends.

Common Diseases

To have a bright, glossy coat, to look well and to perform well, a horse must be kept in good physical condition. Some of the more frequent and debilitating diseases to be on guard against:

Coughs and Colds: Almost always contagious, coughs and colds can spread rapidly through a stable. The horse with a cold should be put in isolation immediately, and the veterinary called at once. The cold itself may not seem important, but such serious illnesses and unsoundnesses as windiness, pneumonia, chronic sinusitis may all result from the untended cold.

Mange and Ringworm: are also highly infectious, and grooming equipment used on infected horses must not be used on healthy horses. The veterinarian will supply treatment for these diseases, and should be treated for they are serious and unsightly.

Azoturia: is a disease which attacks horses that have not been given normal and regular exercise, and are suddenly exposed to vigorous or strenuous work. It is most likely to occur during cool weather. Increased excitability, profuse sweating, and rapid breathing are the first symptoms. Soon, the horse begins to stiffen his hindquarters, drag the hind legs, and knuckle over in the hind fetlocks. Keep the horse standing. Call the veterinarian. Blanket and do not attempt to load up a steep ramp. Aftertreatment consists of light laxative diet and slow return to work.

Colic: Can be detected by the horse's pawing, lying down, rolling and nosing his belly. The danger here, of course, is to help keep the animal from getting cast in his stall. It is often over-eating, eating while fatigued, working too soon after eating, or watering while exhausted. Wind-sucking is another frequent cause of colic. It is well to say here, I think, that all riders should remember that the horse has a small stomach. He should not be fed too much at one time, or fed when he comes in exhausted from a long ride. When horses come in from a hunt, they should be fed a hot bran mash. These simple precautions will prevent a good many cases of colic, but if your horse does develop colic, blanket him, keep him warm, and send for the veterinarian immediately. Consult the veterinarian about feeding after the colic attack. These are the everyday, common diseases that afflict most horses at one time or another. They need not be serious if the veterinarian is sent for and simple remedies, such as those suggested here are applied to keep the animal reasonably comfortable until he gets there.

Stable Vices

The most common stable vices are:

Weaving: A rhythmical shifting of the weight from one foot to the other. As a rule, lack of regular work and exercise is the cause, and a straight stall plus regular exercise may help to correct this habit.

Kicking: A great many horses which never show any inclination to kick anywhere else, somehow acquire the habit of kicking in their stalls. Padding the stall with salvaged mattresses will keep the horse from injuring himself, and hobbling one hind leg for a short period of time will sometimes effect a cure. Use of kicking chain works best.

Cribbing: The edge of the manger or any other projection is grasped between the teeth and gradually bitten away. The habit is, unfortunately, not confined to the stable, but may be practiced whenever the opportunity offers. A smooth finished stall in which there is nothing to offer a toothhold, or the use of a cribbing strap, which compresses the larynx when the head is flexed, but causes the horse no discomfort when he is not indulging in this vice, are the two ways to stop cribbing.

Measuring the Horse

The height of a horse is measured in hands, and a hand is four inches. The measuring stick is placed against the highest point of the withers, with the crossbar resting firmly on the withers and the upright perpendicular. A good height for a hunter is sixteen hands.

A horse's *bone* measurement is the circumference of the middle of the fore cannon region. A horse's bone is measured in inches. Seven inches is a small bone measurement in any horse over 14/2, and nine inches is an exceptional measurement even in a seventeen hand horse. The bone measurement for the average sixteen hand hunter should be about 8½ inches. Bone measurement is important. A horse with good bone has a better than average chance of standing up under the shock and concussion to which the hunter and jumper are exposed.

Age Determination

Determining a horse's age is something else that is better left to the veterinarian. If you have a thoroughbred horse, with papers, you won't have to worry about his age. If you are buying a half or three-quarters bred horse, the vet who passes him for soundness will verify his age. Other than that, a quick rule-of-thumb method for determining the age of a horse is as follows:

At Five: The horse has a full mouth, with all his cups.

At Six: He loses the cups in the centrals.

At Seven: The cups in the laterals are shallow or have disappeared. The seven-year notch appears at the upper corner incisor.

At Eight: The corner cups begin to disappear although they may remain as a shallow cup until about eleven years of age. The dental star usually appears in front of the enamel ring as a rather long, faint yellow, transverse line.

At Ten: Galvayne's groove is distinct and the teeth are becoming more triangular.

At Fifteen: Galvayne's groove is halfway through the corner teeth, and the angle of incidence starts.

At Twenty-Two: Galvayne's groove is extending the length of the tooth, the dental star is large and distinct, and the angle of incidence is pronounced.

But the art of estimating a horse's age accurately cannot be learned from a book, and, as I said before, it is something better left to the experts.

Carl Klein

PART IV

Veterinary Preparation of the Horse and Maintenance of Condition During Competition

By Dr. Joseph C. O'Dea, D.V.M.

THE show horse is an athlete and like the athlete must be prepared to play the game. Its education and coaching may be the best, but if its physical condition is faulty, its ability to win is precluded.

In our selection of mounts for competition, we first perform a searching examination with particular attention to legs, feet, eyes, mouth, respiratory apparatus, and heart.

The feet are usually examined in cooperation with the attending blacksmith and a joint decision is reached regarding the shoeing. A good veterinarian and a good blacksmith will agree. It is only when one or the other is deficient in his knowledge of the horse's foot and the horse's action that controversy arises. If there is a question concerning any condition in the legs or feet, x-rays are taken to assist in the diagnosis, and, more important, in the prognosis.

Most veterinarians are particularly adverse to hoof preparations that are composed of grease, wax, or other water repellent substances. Pack the feet with clay, or if you must use something to make the hooves shine, a mixture of one part of glycerine to *at least* four parts of water is satisfactory. Glycerine is soothing and softening and is miscible with water. Do not use pure glycerine—undiluted glycerine will draw moisture out of the hoof.

Eyes are checked for sight, accommodation for light, the Purkinje-Sanson images, adhesions, opacities, signs of periodic ophthalmia, intra-ocular pressure, and the normal functioning of the naso-lacrimal duct.

The mouth is examined for bite, sharp teeth and loose teeth, cracked or abscessed teeth, ulcers on the tongue, lips, bars and cheek. Floating and cutting, when necessary, is done without delay. The cause of ulcerations is determined and removed, and the ulcers treated. A saturated solution of Copper Sulfate applied with an artist's brush is better than anything else for the purpose. "Wolf teeth" rarely cause any trouble, but can be easily removed if necessary. Loose or offending deciduous (milk) teeth are likewise easily removed.

The heart is examined in the usual clinical fashion and its efficiency measured by its accommodation for exercise of varying intensities. If additional information is required, electrocardiographs are made. The respiratory apparatus and function is examined in comparable fashion.

When horses have passed these tests, we then take blood samples which are analyzed for the following:

1. Red blood cell count
2. White cell count—differential count
3. % of hemoglobin
4. Icteric index

There is no reason to have the samples run for Calcium or Phosphorous for one sample of either is of no significance. If there is some indication of faulty Calcium-Phosphorous metabolism, we require that a series of tests be taken over a period of time and the composite results used in our clinical evaluation.

The fecal (manure) examinations for internal parasites are made of composite samples. Sometimes several samplings are made in a fortnight. The total results of several composite samples give a much clearer indication of the degree of infestation than any single sample.

The present treatment is to administer Parvex via stomach tube at the rate of one ounce for each 200 pounds of body weight. Parvex is a combination of Carbon-disulfide and Piperazine and is effective on bots and ascarids and the small strongyles. It has not been very efficient for the removal of the Strongylus vulgaris, the real demon of the parasites in the adult horse. For this reason, we administer a suspension of phenothiazine via tube several days later. This procedure has proven very effective. The animals are starved only overnight. Much of the colic experienced in worming in previous years was due in part to the excessive period of starvation that the animal was caused to undergo prior to treatment. Have your horse's feces checked periodically or worm him as needed. If you cannot get the feces checked, worm him every six weeks or so while he is on the show circuit. All horses have worms all the time. The problem is to keep them under control by keeping the relative numbers down. For the purposes of this discussion, we will not enter into the field of feeding, except to render the following suggestions: 1. That the hay be at least 40% alfalfa and/or clover, and be of good green color. 2. That the feeding of bran be kept at the lowest possible level required to keep the manure of proper consistency. 3. That instead of oil meal or linseed oil, corn oil be used to help condition the animal and to make his coat shine. A tablespoonful can be fed at each feeding. Mazola oil is very satisfactory for this purpose. 4. A good supplement is good insurance. There are many good ones and many bad ones on the market. My farm manager suggests Dugravet, made by the Taft Laboratories of New Haven, Conn. Controlled experiments at our farm have proven its worth.

I must admonish you to take it very easy on youngsters under five, especially the big, precocious types. The horse, as you know, is not mature until he is past five. That fact, coupled with the artificial life which the travel on the show circuit forces upon him, results in an upset metabolism and disturbed growth of bone, and irreparable damage results. Some of the saddest sights I have seen have been at Harrisburg and the Garden, when willing, handsome youngsters enter the ring with the telltale nod of the splint, the osslet, the bad foot, the spongy suspensory ligament, the result of a summer of forced work on the show circuit.

Unaccountable loss of condition or performance on the show circuit may be due to specific conditions.

Anemia: Can be usually corrected by the administration of vitamin B_{12}—2000 Mcg simultaneously with injectable iron. Tonics containing some copper and cobalt also helpful. Liver extract. Bloodworms under control.

Low serum protein: Several supplements are available which contain the essential protein fractions (essential amino acids). Injectable products can be administered by a veterinarian when necessary.

Nervousness and loss of appetite: Thiamine (Vitamin B_1). Best to use vitamin B complex with extra B_1 added. Injectable or as a food supplement. Bitter tonics. Tranquilizers during shipment.

Signs of fatigue: In face of a maximum effort: Injectable Fructose together with B_1 and essential amino acids. B_{12} and iron if necessary. Electrolytes added to drinking water.

The physical condition of *geldings* is sometimes helped by the administration of Testosterone, or a combination of Testosterone and stilbesterol.

Pain Killers and Tranquilizers

By Dr. Joseph C. O'Dea, D.V.M.

In recent years many efficient pain killers have been produced and many products used for the relief of the pain of arthritis have been put on the market. (Arthritis—inflammation of a joint.)

Some of these products work very well in the treatment of horses and because of their efficiency for certain lamenesses, they have been over used and indiscriminately used and some horses have suffered irreparable damage.

In this group is the product Butazolidine, a fine, useful drug when properly used for the relief of pain from arthritis, bursitis, etc. However, the nature of the drug may sometimes cause circulatory, cardiac and digestive upsets and the use of the drug without proper veterinary care is "madness" Patients must be selected and the size of the dose kept to the minimum.

If you have a problem, consult your veterinarian—don't ruin your horse by "slipping him a pill" just for that one class.

Tranquilizers have also received much publicity in recent years. Much has yet to be learned about their use in horses. Their use in the show ring, hunting field, or for breaking purposes is to my mind an improper use of the drugs and should be discouraged. Their proper use is during shipment, especially by air, in certain diseases such as tetanus, hysteria and in preparation for treatment or after surgery.

Three products, Thorazine, Sparine, and Rauwolfia, have been used successfully on horses. For my own purpose the most satisfactory results have

been obtained through the use of Sparine administered intramuscularly by a veterinarian.

The use of the Tranquilizers is a job for the veterinarian. *Don't experiment.* The use of Tranquilizers in horses is still in the experimental stage. The availability of pain killers, tranquilizers and other modern drugs poses a great problem for horsemen, horse purchasers, veterinarians and horse shows.

I am sure that either or both of these drugs will be used to sell unsound and fractious horses. They have been and are being used in the show ring. The unruly working hunter of this morning's class was "just a lamb" in this afternoon's hack class. The eliminated "cripple" in the 4 P.M. preliminary won the stake class at 9 P.M. and jogged as "sound as a bell of brass." And what can and should be done about it? Is there any sport in showing a fine young, well schooled horse to be beaten by a medicated, tranquilized, normally erratic cast off? It can and does happen.

I don't have an answer—but if an answer isn't found, the unethical use of our new drugs can cause a big problem in the horse show world.

SECTION FIVE

The Rider Expert

Part I

THE EMPLOYMENT OF CAVALETTIS by Bertalan de Nemethy, Coach, U.S.E.T. 111

Part II

FLEXIONS AND COLLECTIONS 114

JUMPING 120

F.E.I. 123

Part III

THE THREE DAY EVENT by Brig. Gen. John T. Cole, U.S.E.T. 125

Part IV

ANALYZING JUMPING COURSES by William Steinkraus, Captain, U.S.E.T. 129

TIME CLASSES by Frank Chapot, U.S.E.T. 143

Part V

THE OLYMPIC GAMES by Maj. Gen. Guy V. Henry, U.S. Olympic Equestrian Committee 145

George Morris
Member of U.S.E.T.

Hugh Wiley
Member of U.S.E.T.

THE RIDER EXPERT

PART I

The Employment of Cavalettis

By Bertalan de Nemethy, Coach, U.S.E.T.

UP to a certain height of fences, jumping is a natural instinct for most horses. (Even the foal will frequently jump small natural obstacles in the paddock.) In employing his natural instincts, the negotiation of obstacles is usually associated in the horse's mind with increase in speed, and consequently it is a relatively easy matter to school horses to race over hurdles; indeed, the horse with ability and courage will jump a really big fence even when very green, if galloping fast enough.

The requirements of modern show-jumping are very different from those of the race track, however. The gradual development of the standards of show-jumping has reached a point at which it is now necessary to employ truly thoughtful and regular training to augment and develop the horse's jumping mechanism if he is to be a winner in the show-ring. Speed is not enough to cope with modern show-ring courses—we must develop the horse's ability to use himself in every way.

In other words, we must teach the horse:

1. To concentrate on where it puts it legs while jumping.
2. To learn how to relax the muscles of the back and neck while jumping, for therein lies the most efficient utilization of the jumping mechanism.
3. To learn how to find the proper take-off spot for all kinds of fences, both broad and high.
4. To preserve balance and impulsion both on the shortened stride and the lengthening stride in the approach and landing.

The most effective way of accomplishing all of these aims lies in the employment of varying forms of cavalettis. The most useful form of cavaletti for these purposes will be found to be rather heavy poles some 5 to 6 feet long, with a maximum height of 8 inches.

It is best to begin by teaching the horse to negotiate a single pole at both a walk and a trot without changing the rhythm of its gait. Certain horses can

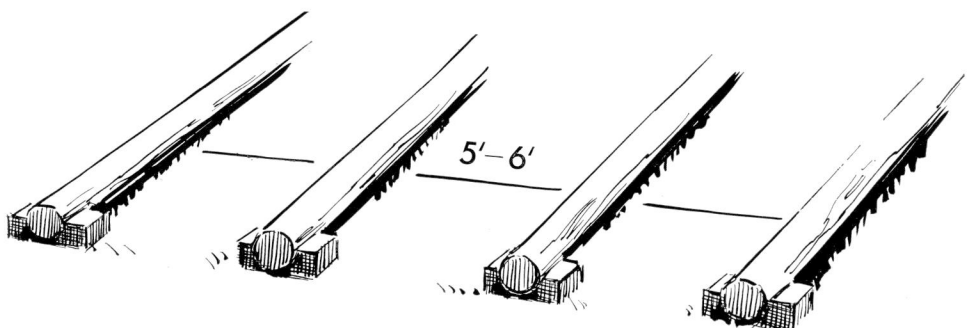

learn to do this after only a few attempts, while those with more difficult dispositions will require a considerably longer period. However, one should not attempt to negotiate series of two, three or four cavalettis until the single rail can be done correctly.

In arranging multiple cavalettis, the spacing will vary according to:

1. The general structure and size of the horse
2. Its length of stride (ordinary trot)
3. Its particular temperament.

The distance will average between five and six feet, but adjustments should be made for each horse individually as is necessary. Once the horse has learned to negotiate cavalettis set to accommodate his stride, the trainer can begin the work of correction, by working to shorten the excessively long stride, and working to lengthen the restricted stride. In general, he will know the purposes of the exercise are being achieved when the horse is able to negotiate the cavalettis without changing his rhythm, with a complete relaxation of back and neck muscles, a low and well-stretched neck, an alert expression watching the cavalettis, and when the steps fall evenly in the center of the space between the cavalettis.

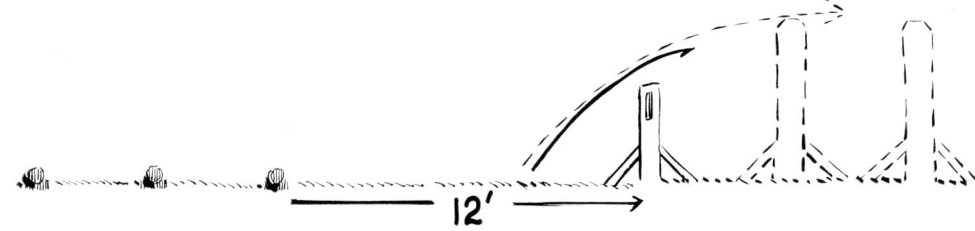

When this level of performance has been reached, the horse can be asked to jump a small fence (at a maximum height of 2′) placed about twelve feet beyond the last cavaletti in the series. This fence should be jumped in exactly the same rhythm that is used to trot through the cavaletti, only the force of the last stride being a little greater.

Once the horse's rhythm is sufficiently stabilized over the single, simple fence, innumerable variants can be employed to deal with particular problems. Higher, broader fences can be used to develop a willingness to extend, and stretch in the air; moving the fence closer can help to develop the horse's ability to collect itself, and fully utilize its hocks during the thrust-off. As a means of verifying the fact that the horse's rhythm stays unchanged, and in order to help it to recognize the proper take-off point by itself, the last cavaletti can be removed (or placed first), thus leaving a longer open space before the take-off. This technique can be extended, and varied as to distance; small "combinations" can be erected following the cavaletti and the trainer's own powers of analysis and imagination will suggest many ways of varying the form of cavalettis to deal with particular difficulties.

PART II

Flexions and Collections

Direct Flexion makes it easy for a horse to displace weight from his forehand to his haunches. The same is true of collection at increased speeds. The faculty of being able to displace weight from forehand to haunches is invaluable in a hunter when making sharp turns at rapid speeds. A horse whose weight is on his haunches can make a sharp turn safely, whereas one whose weight is on his forehand may cross his front legs and go down.

Lateral Flexion differs from Direct Flexion in that the jaw and poll yield on the same side of the horse's head. This effect is obtained by the same methods as that used for *direct flexion,* but instead of using the direct rein aid to accomplish flexion, the indirect rein is used, displacing the horse's weight laterally, or diagonally. Lateral flexion is particularly useful for horses with extremely bad mouths. Such horses often put up strong resistance against flexion, but lateral flexion, in which, first one side, then the other side, of a horse's mouth is flexed, will sometimes fool such an animal into yielding, and gradually improve his mouth.

Flexion and Collection

"Flexion" and "Collection" are rather overpowering terms that describe the effect produced by the action of reins and legs to make a horse flex his jaw or his poll, helping to develop a good mouth, putting him on the bit, where he can be made to respond to the slightest command.

Any horse can have at least a fair mouth. Most horses can have good mouths, if their owners and riders are willing to take the time and trouble to mouth them *before asking them to jump*. But even if the damage has already been done, some knowledge of the proper way to flex your horse, to collect him and to put him on the bit, can overcome much, if not all of the damage of the early lack of training.

To a good saddle horse, of course, flexion and collection are essential. For a hunter, they are simply a means to the end of having a responsive, easily controlled horse.

The purpose of *flexion* is to teach the horse to flex his jaw and his poll and come back to the rider, instead of hanging in the rider's hands, boring, or fighting the pressure of the bit. All horses should be taught to flex, since it improves the horse's head carriage and makes him more easily controlled. There are two kinds of flexion: Direct flexion, and lateral flexion. Flexion that is produced directly, by the application of a *direct rein;* and flexion that is produced laterally by the application of an *indirect rein*.

In *all* of riding, the legs are used to produce impulsion, and the hands—via the rein aids—to regulate that impulsion. Therefore, in flexions, the hands collect and control; the legs impel; the hands again come into action to distribute that impulsion either directly or laterally.

And too, as in all phases of riding, there is an easy way to teach a horse to flex, and a more complicated way. Even the comparative beginner can be taught the easy way to flex his horse. I think you will be rather surprised and very pleased with the result which even a few minutes of flexing your horse in a simple, elementary way will produce.

To Produce Direct Flexion

A. This is teaching the horse to be on the bit, or to move into the bit and take a normal feel of it with an extended neck. To do this, the rider takes feel of his horse's mouth, the legs close against the horse's sides to force him to move into the bit while the closed hands prevent him from moving forward.

B. As soon as the horse has moved up into the bit and flexed, or relaxed his jaw, the rider relaxes his hands and legs instantly, thereby rewarding the horse for his obedience.

This is a fairly simple exercise, easily learned and quickly mastered. In the beginning, it is best to practice this exercise while standing still or walking.

C. If the rider is not sufficiently skilled to be able to *feel* the exact instant at which his horse's mouth has yielded and flexed, then he should watch his horse's mouth in a mirror. It is essential that the horse be rewarded the instant he has yielded, or this exercise will quickly boomerang and create a mouth problem instead of solving one. This exercise is best practiced when asking the horse to decrease speed from a walk to a standstill.

D. After the horse has been taught to flex his jaw, he must be taught how to flex his poll. This is done with "Fixed hands," which are hands set to increase pressure on the horse's mouth, with the legs closed on the horse, and pressure does not relax until the horse has yielded. The moment the horse flexes his jaw and then his poll, the fingers *relax* and the horse is *thereby* rewarded.

This exercise is more difficult than the two previous which I have mentioned, because the rider takes a stronger hold, or feel of his horse's mouth, instead of merely establishing contact with the horse's mouth. Hands and legs both act strongly, and since the result produced will be equally strong, it is not necessary but imperative that the rider's aids be sufficiently well coordinated so that he feels the exact moment his horse has yielded, and can yield pressure at the same time.

Collection

The first step toward collection is flexion, as I have described and outlined it. Once the horse has been put on the bit, and taught to flex his jaw and poll for longer periods at a time, he is said to be *collected,* and "In hand," or "On the hand," all riding terms which mean the same thing.

A. When a horse is behind the bit he is out of control.

B. When a horse is behind the bit, the rider has the feeling of having "nothing in his hands." To compensate, the rider tends to get ahead of the horse, especially when jumping, but even when posting to the trot. The further ahead the rider gets in this vicious circle, the further behind the horse gets, and very often, when they reach the jump, they part company altogether, each going his different way.

Unless the horse is on the bit, or on the rider's hands, he can neither give nor receive signals. He can drop his head and quit at the last minute. He can run out. He can dog along at the walk or the trot, requiring the constant use of the rider's legs, spurs and voice to keep him going.

The horse is first collected by the strong use of the direct rein and the active leg. He practices, first, the collected walk, which differs from the normal walk by a decrease in speed from approximately four miles an hour to three miles an hour, the higher action compensating for the loss of speed. A horse's normal trotting speed is six to eight miles an hour, while his collected trot is closer to four or five miles an hour. His normal canter is ten to twelve miles an hour, while his collected canter is between six to eight miles an hour. The stride is shorter, the action higher and more animated.

The rider should not ask his horse to remain collected for long periods at a time. Be sure to reward him at frequent intervals by letting him extend his walk and travel with a floating rein.

All horses should be taught to flex, because it makes them easier to ride and to control. *Few* hunters should be asked for exaggerated collection because it makes them higher-spirited, more anxious, and might, in time, affect the manner and the quality of their jump and their way of going.

The Flying Changes of the Lead

When moving from a right lead to a left lead, the following aids are used to effect a flying change, after the horse is collected:

1. The left indirect rein is applied in front of the withers. The right rein is a direct rein, and a passive one.
2. The right leg becomes active, displacing the horse's haunches, forcing him to take the left lead.

The difference between the flying change of lead and the ordinary change of lead is, of course, the speed and smoothness with which the different aids must be applied, so that while each is applied separately, the effect is that of having been applied simultaneously. It is almost impossible, watching a skilled horseman make a flying change of lead, to see the different aids being applied. For that reason, such high-school work should not be tried until the aids are working automatically with no conscious thought on the part of the rider as to their sequence.

The Use of Legs To Ride Your Horse

With the coordination of your hands either with a feel or a fixed hand your horse can be made to move either forward or backward entirely by the use of your legs. (Try it.)

Use of the Aids for the Extended Trot

When the horse is on the bit and doing a collected trot he can be taught to extend the trot. The rider's legs demand greater impulsion so that extension of hind legs drives the forehand to its greatest extension. As the horse extends, collection should be abandoned, light contact on horse's mouth for support giving horse as much liberty of neck as possible.

The Use of the Aids for the Two-Track

The horse is said to be two-tracking when he moves off the line of movement obliquely. The horse's head is turned in the direction of the movement; the outside legs pass over and in front of the inside legs. The aids for the two-track: Right indirect rein in rear of withers, left leg active, displacing the haunches in the direction of movement. The left rein is a passive rein. The direction in which the horse moves at the two-track should not exceed forty-five degrees to his original position.

Jumping

1. Moving into the approach, the rider is in a three point contact. Notice the line from horse's mouth to elbow. Legs are active.

2. The take-off. The horse thrusts the rider forward and upward, but the line from horse's mouth to rider's elbow continues unbroken. This is jumping out of hand, but should attempted only after the seat is sufficiently secure to permit the hands to work independent of the body.

3. The flight. Again, notice the line from mouth to elbow.

4. The landing, with the flexed-in ankles, the inner bones of the knees and the ankles receiving the shock, enabling the rider to keep his position easily and maintain the unbroken line from mouth to elbow.

5. The rider sinks down in his saddle and continues the contact with his horse's mouth.

By the time the rider is ready for advanced jumping, his hands should move with the horse's mouth automatically. The eyes should have formed the habit of looking forward, focusing on either the next jump or the next turn. His heels should be down.

If, however, the rider finds his hands rotating backward, and interfering with his horse's mouth, he should not hesitate to return to the earlier jumping forms and exercises for releasing at the jump with contact on the horse's crest with his hands. I have often thought that "pride goeth before a fall" describes those riders who are too proud to reach for the mane or to put their hands up before a jump, but not too proud to come back on their horse's mouth in mid-air, punishing the horse's mouth.

Since the term "jumping out of hand" is so vastly misunderstood, let me take a minute to explain what jumping out of hand really means. A rider may be said to be "jumping out of hand" when his security and balance in the saddle is such that he is able to maintain a direct line from the horse's mouth to the rider's elbow, before, during and after the jump, with the same amount of pressure on the horse's mouth.

Broken Line: A broken line is not bad in itself if the rider's hands haven't dropped. This not only breaks the line from mouth to elbow, but in dropping, brings the bit against the bars of the horse's mouth and jabs him almost as severely as though the rider had faulted in the other extreme and comes back on his horse's mouth. The line from mouth to elbow is maintained not because it looks well, but because while the line is maintained, the rider's body is necessarily in the correct position and the horse's mouth is not interfered with in any way. That is why we strive for this line.

Shock Absorbers

Another important point that comes into use in this final stage of jumping is the rider's shock absorbers. His shock absorbers are his ankles and the inner bones of his knees. When the ankles are flexed in and the heels are depressed, the shock of the horse's landing will be absorbed by the ankles and by the inner knee bones, which are kept in light contact with the horse's sides. These shock absorbers are important in many ways: they reduce the shock of landing and so make it possible for the rider to maintain his position in the saddle. When the shock absorbers are not used, the jar can change the rider's whole position in the saddle.

But, jumping out of hand is the goal toward which all riders are working. It enables the rider to ride a course of jumps without wings with less danger of runouts. The rider can now attempt more difficult horses, because he is able to use all of his aids in controlling his horse.

This ideal form of jumping is something that anyone with the will and the patience to learn can master. It is impossible for any rider to jump out of hand if the rider is either mentally or physically hanging back in the saddle. The rider must be confident, and he can be confident only if he has put in enough riding hours to build up his security in the saddle.

F.E.I.

Usually, when competing at an American horse show, you ride under the rules of the American Horse Show Association. However, more and more shows are putting in classes that are ridden under F.E.I. rules. This is what they are and what they mean.

F.E.I. rules are the regulations made by the Federation Equestre Internationale, the largest horse show governing body in the world. F.E.I. rules are very simple. An element of time is introduced along these lines: In the first round of each jumping class there is a time limit. Any horse going evenly and well will complete the course comfortably within this time limit. If he exceeds the time limit, he will be penalized one quarter fault for each second over the limit. In addition, he will be penalized: 4 faults for a knock down whether in front or behind, 3 faults for the first refusal, 6 faults for the second, elimination third. In the case of a fall, the rider may remount and continue the course, but time will run on throughout, and there will be a penalty of eight faults. Ticks are not penalized in any way.

Jump-offs are judged on the basis of time and jumping faults as follows.

1. If one horse has a clean round in slow time and another horse makes a fault in faster time, the clean round wins.

2. If two horses have an equal number of faults, the one with faster time wins.

Why are classes judged under F.E.I. rules, important for American horse shows? For this reason: as we all know and regret, the Army Horse Show Team, which has carried our flag into one set of Olympic Games after another, no longer exists. Olympic competition must now depend on civilian effort. Everyone's cooperation and help both morally and financially are needed. To prepare a team for the next Olympics both horses and riders must be accustomed to the conditions under which they will be obliged to compete, and this takes hours, days, months and years of hard work.

What Judges Look for in F.E.I. Three Day Event Schooling

At the Halt

The horse is in hand, standing squarely on four legs, ready to obey the rider.

A Free Walk at 4 Miles Per Hour

The horse is extended and relaxed in hand. His steps should be equal and deliberate, and in cadence.

The change of pace and gaits should always be executed swiftly and promptly as they are called for.

The horse should always be in hand and very light, responding easily as he is circled, or changes of direction are executed. There must be no abrupt movements.

When two tracking, the head and neck should be going in the direction of movement.

Changes of lead in the air should be done in the period of suspension when the horse's four feet are off the ground.

The use of the voice as in clucking is forbidden.

John Zimerman for *Sports Illustrated*. 1956 Time Inc.

PART III

The Three Day Event

By Brig. Gen. John T. Cole, U.S.E.T.

AFTER World War II the Duke of Beaufort is reputed to have said, "This is the hunting man's game", referring, of course, to the Three Day Event of the Olympic Games. If his remark provided the impetus to the hunting folk of England to get behind this event and push, His Grace has indeed a strong and influential following. For the British hunting fraternity certainly has embraced the Three Day Event with a fervor which has carried British men and women to the front in international competition in this searching test of horse and rider.

Since the advent of Equestrian Sports as a compulsory part of Olympic Games (Stockholm, 1912) the Three Day Event has been known as the Complete Test of the hunter or military horse. Actually, as the military dominated the Equestrian Sports of nearly all nations up to World War II, the contest became known as "The Military". In Europe, today, most horsemen refer to the combined training competitions as "The Military Event". Having been a military man in the Cavalry arm for more years than I care to divulge, it has been my good fortune to have seen many of the world's great hunters and their military counterparts. The only difference I have seen between the tops of both groups is that the military horses showed evidence of more painstaking and demanding training. By eliminating the horse from the military picture, our government has placed the continuance of this best of all equestrian contests squarely in the laps of our hunting people. So what is in this package that the authorities have so nonchalantly tossed into space? As the name of the event implies, three separate competitions have been blended into an overall determination of excellence.

The primary step is to determine who has the best trained, best moving, the most obedient, the most flexible, and all the other qualifications that go into a potentially great field horse. Hence, the initial competition is a simple Dressage Test. Herein, the horse is required to execute a series of rigidly prescribed movements on a 20 metre by 60 metre track. Accuracy, obedience, grace, alertness, promptness and perfection of cadence are the key words which govern the allegedly simple presentation. Only movements which the horse, with sound basic training executes as routine responses to daily demand, are required. All gaits are tested both slightly collected and extended. Great emphasis and weight are placed on the horse's impulsion, and the smoothness and promptness of the transition back and forth from ordinary to extended use of gaits.

To score well in this day of testing, the horse must be well trained to move as an athlete. Movements must be done correctly, not approximately correctly, and his entire attention must be given to his rider.

The skill of the rider is of equal importance. He must have the physical skill which enables him to transmit his will to the horse without any outward indication that he is making a demand on him. The rider must have the fine sensitivity which enables him to anticipate any resistance and break it up before it occurs. This same sensitivity enables him to prepare his horse secretly for the next movement, without showing effect until the instant of execution.

A good horse with a bad rider is a "razor in a monkey's hand". Only the proper rider on the proper horse can succeed.

Having determined the horse's ability to perform the first phase, the second day is designed to test his speed and endurance.

The so-called "Cross Country" Phase consists of a total of 22 miles in 119 minutes divided as follows:

1. At zero hour, the horse starts on 4½ miles of Roads and Trails. Time allowance: 30 minutes.

2. Immediately thereafter comes 2¼ miles of steeplechase. Time allowance: 6 minutes.
3. Next is another road and trail test, this time for 9 miles. Time allowance: 60 minutes.

4. Without rest the cross country test of about 5 miles with 34 obstacles must be completed. Time allowance: 17 minutes.

The jumps are limited to 3′ 11″ in height and 8′ spread. Generally the ground is varied, leaning towards the rugged side. Jumps are solid and many are placed in awkward spots, which require big and courageous jumps from a great horse to come through with his feet on the ground.

5. As the cross country comes to an end, the finish line is about a mile and a quarter away. Time allowed: 6 minutes.

In scoring this second phase, all over-time is penalized, as are all falls, refusals or run-outs. Bonus points can be made on the steeplechase and cross country (Parts 2 and 4) only, by being under the time allowed. Factors such as exceeding the time limit (1-1/5 time—allowed on roads and trails, double time allowed on steeplechase and cross country), 4 disobediences at an obstacle, cutting a flag or uncorrected error in course, will eliminate a contestant.

To show that a horse is versatile, and ready to go again after the tests in the second phase, the third and final phase takes place in the form of Stadium Jumping, on the final day. Here, the horse is judged under F.E.I. rules for Table A, with faults converted to penalty points to give desired weight in comparison with the scoring of the first two phases of the contest. All penalty marks are balanced against bonus points, and the contestant with the fewest penalty points (total) wins.

The Three Day Event is surely a contest which brings out the best qualities of man and horse. The horse must be naturally courageous. He must be sound and be so constructed that he is not predisposed to joint injuries under hard work. Great endurance and fine galloping ability are essentials. His gaits must be straight, long and elastic. There must be no question of his jumping ability. Though, by dimension, fences are relatively small, by placement many become enormous obstacles requiring a bold, big and certain jump. A fine appearance never hurt any horse. Last, but far from least, a level head is essential. One cannot afford a blow-up. An ideal middle weight hunter pretty nearly fits this description. The rider must be a worker. He cannot weigh much over the prescribed 165 pounds. He must have natural talent and must augment his gift by constant study and application. His heart must match that of his horse. He must have a vast knowledge to get his horse fit without burning him out. He must have experience that has taught him to rate his horse and to judge just how much his horse has left, particularly in his cross country phase.

Do not these requirements of character and physical ability in both horse and rider point straight to the hunting field? Definitely the Three Day Event is the hunting man's game.

PART IV

Analyzing Jumping Courses

By WILLIAM STEINKRAUS, Captain, U.S.E.T.

TWO riders are sitting on their horses at the in-gate waiting to perform in a class over fences. Both have about the same degree of skill as riders, and their horses are very nearly on a par. But one of them can outperform the other 80% of the time; and he does it, in effect, before either one jumps a fence. Why is this so? A leading professional show-rider once told me, "you don't have to outride everyone else to win a class—you can *out-think* most of them". He was pointing up the fact that in practice it is not necessarily the best rider that wins, it is the best *competitor*. Nor is the best competitor necessarily the most aggressive, or the one with the fewest butterflies in his stomach—he is characterized mainly by his ability to deliver, in the ring, the highest proportion of the skills and capacities he and his horse possess.

The good competitor accomplishes this because he has learned to anticipate the problems he is going to encounter in the ring, and he knows in

Course for Olympic Games at Stockholm 1956

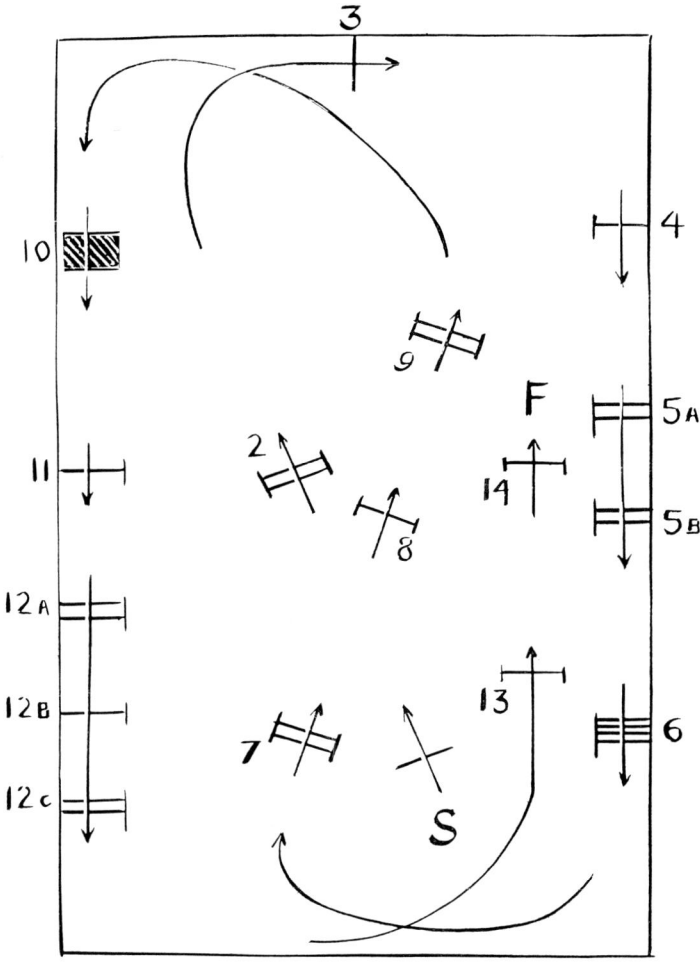

advance how he is going to deal with them. He and his horses may both have real weaknesses—but the good competitor will avoid exposing most of them. I have heard it said that "all this business about figuring out strides and distances is much too complicated, and too much trouble", and unquestionably many exhibitors get by without ever thinking about it. But the higher the standard of the competition and the more difficult the courses, the less one can afford the luxury of simply waiting to see what happens in the ring. When the courses become very difficult, as in the Olympic Games, an understanding of the precise nature of their difficulty is a pre-condition of self protection as well as a pre-condition for success.

Basically, of course, understanding the jumper course is not a difficult or complicated matter; the essential facts one needs are simple to the point of being self-evident. As stated in the AHSA rule book in the section on courses they are: "obstacles are difficult to the degree that their form conflicts with the natural arc of the horse's jump", and "distances between fences are awkward to the degree that they require the horse to alter his normal stride." The natural arc of the horse's jump and the length of his stride will vary, of course, with the conformation of the particular horse, the type of fence, and the rate of speed and amount of impulsion being used. However, relatively little observation is needed to establish the general norms and the range of variation.

Probably the best way to develop judgement about the length of strides and average take-off and landing distances is to set up various kinds of fences on a stretch of level ground that can be raked and smoothed after every jump. In this way one can experiment with different approach speeds and different take-offs, and check visually the actual distances that resulted. It is always profitable to while away some of the time between classes at the shows by concentrating entirely on the footfall of horses in negotiating various fences and combinations, however, and much can be learned in this way.

Armed with a general knowledge of the range of variation of strides and take-off and landing distances, one will be able to anticipate most of the trouble spots on the average course simply by pacing off the distances and relating them to the average horse. (These measurements pertain principally, of course, to combinations and the shorter distances; fences that are farther than five strides away from each other can generally be ridden as individual obstacles, since the rider will have time and space to make considerable adjustments in his approach between fences.) In this connection it is a great convenience to learn the length of one's own stride, or to find out how much of a stretch is required to take a 3' step. In practice, most riders walk courses in terms of an average horse's stride of 12', which is four paces.

Even when riders are not permitted to inspect the course on foot it is almost always possible to watch a few horses jump before performing yourself, and even a horse or two can give you an idea as to how the in-and-outs and shorter distances will probably ride. In judging from other horses one must always remember to compensate for the horse that takes an abnormally long or short stride, whether you are watching him—or about to ride him.

Aside from the difficulties that involve distance, the rider's principal concern will be with the turns, footing, construction of fences, and occasionally, direction of the sun. Generally he will want to plan his turns with an eye to the previous fence and the next fence as well as the turning point itself; he will always select the better footing if there is a difference between one panel and the adjoining one; he will check both sides of a fence, and jump the one that is most securely fixed if there is a difference; and he will make sure that his proposed course will not head him directly into a setting sun (or other distraction) which might be avoided by taking the fence at a slight angle.

Having thus analyzed where the course's particular difficulties will

probably lie, the rider must relate them to the particular capacities and degree of schooling of the horse he is to ride. A good deal of judgement is needed in this; some horses have a special talent for jumping accurately and smoothly with a rather short take-off, while others may stand back an extra foot or two quite comfortably. The "long" horse may tend to look awkward or jump less cleanly from a take-off that would be only a trifle short for the average horse, while another may jump a little cleaner if asked to reach a little for its fences. Other factors that must be considered are tendencies to gain or lose speed on a course, the inclination to "flatten out" or refuse to come back if asked to stand back too often, and so on for almost as many variations as there are horses. The main point is that to anticipate a problem in terms of a particular horse is very often to be able to avoid it, by planning the ride in a way that will circumvent or minimize the horse's weakness.

Even before the rider enters the ring, he should have a clear idea of how he wants to ride his course if possible. Plans being what they are, it will not always be possible to execute the plan as desired, and the rider should have given some thought to alternatives for the key spots of the course. Let's say, for example, that one has decided to jump a long in-and-out in one

stride, assuming a normal "in". Should the horse meet the first fence badly and land very short, will there be room for two short strides, or must the rider insist on an even longer take-off? His decision will have to be made instantly, and it is more likely to be the correct one if the possibility has been considered previously. Nothing is worse than starting to ride a course without knowing what one intends to do at some crucial point—but it is equally bad to stick blindly to a plan that is no longer valid or realistic.

In stating that the rider must know what he wants to do before he enters the ring we do not mean to imply that he must plan to do *everything*. The scope of the plan will vary considerably according to the rider's and his horse's experience. Thus the skilled professional may make virtually every decision for the novice horse, while the novice rider will leave many decisions to the "old stager". In either case it is important that the practice is consistent, and definite. One must never start to decide for a horse, and then desert him; timid, half-hearted decisions are almost worse than none at all.

Up to this point we have been discussing the analysis of courses from the rider's point of view, and assumed that his examination of the course will reveal what he must do to make the most of his horse. Most often this will not be a very difficult or subtle process, for the problems presented by the course are usually relatively straightforward in this country. It is an extremely stimulating experience, however, to ride a course that has been conceived of as an examination of the horse's and rider's skills and capacities —in other words, a course that is trying to expose your combined weaknesses, just as you are trying to disguise them.

In my opinion, the course used for the Prix des Nations at the 1956 Olympic Equestrian Games in Stockholm was a brilliant example of such a course. In practice, it proved difficult enough to prevent any entry from completing two faultless rounds (though the winners, H. G. Winkler and "Halla", came breathtakingly close)—and yet the distribution of faults showed that this was achieved without laying "traps" for the contestants, or facing them with anything that was unsportsmanlike. Indeed, the two outside lines of fences (see fences 4, 5a, b, 6 and 10, 11, 12a, b, c in the course diagram on page 130), which were really the heart of the course, constituted problems that could be solved not only in one, but in several ways—if the solution was executed perfectly!

For example, it was perfectly possible to make five short strides or four long ones between fences 4 and 5a—the "in" of an unusually long double. The high first rail of the "out" dictated a single stride between 5a and 5b, however. (No horse succeeded in jumping out cleanly after two strides, though there were several attempts.) Thus if the five stride alternative was chosen, a great ability to preserve impulsion within a short stride was required; if the four stride approach was used, a great willingness to "go forward" and ability to stand back with no hesitation were necessary. The

combination was jumped successfully both ways, but almost any slight error in execution—and a moment's doubt by the rider, or a moment's hesitation or resistance by the horse—would show up as a fault at 5b if not sooner.

The opposite outside line was even more interesting, since there was an option between the water and the wall (10 and 11); another option between 11 and 12a; two unavoidably short strides to 12b, and one unavoidably long one to 12c. From 10 to 11 to 12a it was possible to use 4 strides and 4, 5 and 5, 4 and 5 or 5 and 4—but no matter which solution was used, the three-combination was a difficult one, which would again penalize any defect in horse or rider. And this is as it should be in the Olympic Games; the real proof of the excellence of the course is the unquestionable excellence of the horse-rider combinations that finished close to the top.

An intelligent analysis of the jumping course makes the relatively simple one even simpler—but it makes the very difficult one *possible*. And in exercising the combined capacities of your horse and rider, both mental and physical, in the accomplishment of a fair but demanding task lie the greatest pleasures riding can afford.

Bill Steinkraus

Budd

Time Classes

By Frank Chapot, U.S.E.T.

IN all international horse shows, there are a great number of time classes. These classes are of all types, such as, take your own line, fault and out with the competition jumping as many fences as he can in a specified time, table C classes in which seconds are added to the competitor's time for knockdowns and refusals incurred, classes in which the competitor rides two horses and changes horses in the ring, and others. The object of these competitions is to be the fastest horse with the least number of faults which usually means the fastest clean horse. There are many factors to consider when first viewing a time course before riding it. Of these, the most important to me is trying to find the shortest possible route to complete the course. The rider must figure the amount he can cut the turns and jump fences on angles within the limits of his horse's capabilities.

When walking or seeing a course before riding it, a rider finds places on the course which will allow him to leave out a stride between two fences. I mean by this, that if the distance between two fences is such that it can be

ridden in either four long strides or five short strides, the rider will save time by asking his horse to do it in four.

When riding in a time class, you must try to go through the starting timers at the same pace you are to use throughout the course. In most cases it is very difficult to make up time lost in the beginning on any other particular part of the course. Start off with enough speed so that you won't have to increase your pace later on the course to make up for a slow start.

To save time on a course, jump the fences which are immediately followed by a turn in the corner in the direction of the turn, for example, if you have a right turn after a fence, jump the fence in the right corner and be turning when your horse's hindquarters touch the ground.

The position in which you compete in a time class is one of the factors which determine how you will ride that particular competition. The best position to have is last. If you ride after all the other horses have completed, you know the difficulties the other riders have encountered. From this knowledge, you can figure how sharp to cut turns, how sharp to figure angles, and the other number of chances you must take in order to win. When riding early in a time competition, the rider has no alternative but to go all out and to take all possible chances if he expects to win.

Time classes call for horses which are very clever and respond to the rider's aids immediately. The best type of horse for time competition is one that sets himself before his fences and may even have a tendency to be very careful. This type of horse will remain clever and careful even when the rider is driving him forward at a fast pace. The bold going horse that stands way back from his fences and takes long strides will usually be hard to turn sharp and get in trouble when he gets in close.

Time courses usually have many tricky turns and difficult angles which give the rider with the handy horse the advantage over the bold mover that can only make time galloping. The success of General Mariles and Chihuahua II proves this point.

Frank D Chapot

Elaine Werner

PART V

The Olympic Games

By Maj. Gen. Guy V. Henry, U.S. Olympic Equestrian Committee

THE first modern Olympic Games were held in Athens in 1896. They must be held in four-year cycles, or omitted entirely. Those for 1916, 1940, and 1944 were omitted due to war.

The International Olympic Committee is the world's governing body for the Olympic Games. It draws up the general program, designates the country where the next Olympiad will be held, indicates the sports, the standard of amateurism. Its Executive Committee acts as the Jury of Appeal during the Games.

There is a National Olympic Committee in each country.

There is also an International Sports Federation for each sport, which prescribes the rules and regulations for its sport and conduct in the Olympic Games.

These three groups—the International Olympic Committee, the National Olympic Committees and the International Sports Federations—meet intermittently in an Olympic Congress.

The National Olympic Committee of the country to which the Olympic Games are assigned is responsible for the physical plant for the Games. It usually delegates this to an Organizing Committee in one of its cities. This Organizing Committee produces the complete plant and administrative personnel for operation. The International Sports Federations working with their affiliated National Sports Federations, on the other hand, handle the sports. For the equestrian sports, The International Federation is the Federation Equestre Internationale (FEI). The U.S. National Federation is the American Horse Shows Association (AHSA).

The organization for the Pan-American Games closely follows that for the Olympics.

The equestrian events of the Olympic Games are the greatest horse competitions of the world. Racing, polo and other horse events have outstanding contests, but nowhere else are so many countries, or horsemen, represented. No American can realize their importance in the eyes of most countries, nor the official and social courtesies shown the equestrian teams. Since World War II there has been a decrease of cavalry. Prior to that war these teams were composed of military officers, who were the official representatives of their respective countries, and were treated accordingly. With the advent of mixed teams this practice largely continues.

The equestrian events are three in number and were introduced into the Games in 1912, with the United States Army a participant. There have been eight since 1912. The United States has competed in all, and with the possible exception of Sweden, has had the greatest number of entries.

The 1912 and 1920 Olympics showed many deficiencies in the equestrian rules. This led to the founding in 1921 of the now governing body, the Federation Equestre Internationale (FEI). The United States was one of the eight original members. In 1957 nearly 50 nations were affiliated.

As previously stated the equestrian events are three in number: Grand Dressage—Three Day—Grand Prize Jumping. Heretofore each nation could enter three in each event and compete for both individual and team Olympic Victory Medals. Gold first places, silver second, bronze third. To be eligible for a team medal all three riders must complete the course. There are some changes regarding entries and medals being considered for the future.

Grand Dressage

This is the modern version of the equestrian art as practiced by the great masters of past centuries. It is open to both men and women. It is designed to show the obedience, balance, suppleness and perfect lightness of the horse, together with the regularity, straightness and extension of his gaits. The ride requires all the finesse of the equestrian art and includes certain airs approaching high school. Under the controlling influence of the FEI the past divergence of the various European schools has been largely eliminated in this event. The U.S. has entered teams in six of the nine Olympics and won 1 individual silver, 1 team silver, and 1 team bronze Olympic Victory Medals.

Three Day

Prior to the development of radio and efficient aviation, military commanders were dependent for information of the enemy on mounted officer reconnaissance patrols and on gallopers for carrying their messages. Patrols worked well in advance of the Army. Both patrols and gallopers avoided roads, moved across country, frequently at speed, and often engaged in saber or pistol combat. All this required a horse with schooling, endurance, speed, cross-country and jumping ability and a rider with guts. Hence "The Military", "The Complete Event", or the "Three Day", as it is known today, was introduced.

The first day dressage—schooling. The second day—endurance with its steeplechase course for speed, its long cross-country for galloping, jumping and test of determination for both horse and rider, its roads and trails to test the judgement of the rider. The third day—stadium jumping, to see if the horse could carry on after the grueling test of the second day. The U.S. has been very successful in this event with its good thoroughbred horses and determined riders. It has entered all nine Olympics, won 3 individual silver, 2 gold team, 2 bronze team Olympic Victory Medals.

Grand Prix Jumping

This big jumping event, the greatest of the world, open to both men and women, is the glamour contest of the Olympic Games. It is the final contest, held in the great stadium in connection with the colorful and impressive "Closing Ceremonies". Half a million or more spectators and high officials from all nations are there to view it.

Winners of other events have had their chance before, but the first, second and third placed in this event are the last to stand on the dais to receive their gold, silver or bronze Olympic Victory Medals, to have the thrilling and glorious sight of seeing the Games end with their respective national flags raised to the Olympic mast—heard amid the roar of the multitude. Americans twice have had this thrill.

May the students of this book carry on, thus bringing honor to their country and themselves, by mast-heading the Stars and Stripes many times in the equestrian events of the Olympic Games of the future.

Guy V. Henry.